CAT

PRACTICE & REVISION KIT

Advanced Paper 9

Preparing Taxation Computations (Finance Acts 2005)

BPP is the **official provider** of training materials for the ACCA's CAT qualification. This Practice & Revision Kit forms part of a suite of learning tools, which also includes CD-ROMs for tuition and computer based assessment, and the innovative, internet-based 'virtual campus'.

In this January 2006 edition

This Practice and Revision Kit is an essential revision tool for CAT students studying for exams in 2006. Its features include:

- Thorough and reliable updating for **FINANCE ACTS 2005**

- **QUESTIONS WITH HELP** and questions with **HELPING HANDS**

- **QUESTION AND ANSWER BANK** covering the syllabus

- **MARKING GUIDANCE** showing where marks are awarded

- The ACCA's June 2005 and December 2005 papers as **MOCK EXAMS**

FOR JUNE 2006 AND DECEMBER 2006 EXAMS

BPP Professional Education
January 2006

First edition 2004
Third edition January 2006

ISBN 0 7517 2578 1 (Previous ISBN 0 7517 2228 6)

British Library Cataloguing-in-Publication Data
A catalogue record for this book
is available from the British Library

Published by

BPP Professional Education
Aldine House, Aldine Place
London W12 8AW

www.bpp.com

Printed in Great Britain by W M Print
45-47 Frederick Street
Walsall, West Midlands
WS2 9NE

We are grateful to the Association of Chartered Certified Accountants for permission to reproduce the syllabus, the pilot paper and past examination questions of which the Association holds the copyright. The suggested solutions have been prepared by BPP Professional Education.

We are also grateful to the Chartered Institute of Management Accountants and the Association of Accounting Technicians for permission to reproduce past examination questions in this Kit. The suggested answers have been prepared by BPP Professional Education.

Page

BPP PROFESSIONAL EDUCATION

The headings in this checklist/index indicate the main topics of the questions, but questions often cover several different topics. This reflects the approach of the examiner.

BPP PROFESSIONAL EDUCATION

HOW TO USE THIS PRACTICE & REVISION KIT

Aim of this Practice & Revision Kit

> To provide the practice to help you succeed in the examination for Paper 9 *Preparing Taxation Computations*.

To pass the examination you need a thorough understanding in all areas covered by the syllabus and teaching guide.

Recommended approach

- Make sure you are able to answer questions on **everything** specified by the syllabus and teaching guide.

- Attempt **all** of the questions in this Practice & Revision Kit. Each section has at least one **QUESTION WITH HELP** and one question without any help or guidance. Some of the other questions have **HELPING HANDS** which you should use in order to help you answer the question in the best way.

- There are 50 questions in this Practice and Revision Kit.

  - Many questions give feedback on **WHAT THE EXAMINER SAID** where relevant.

  - There is a **MARKING GUIDE** at the end of most questions

  - There is a mark allocation for each question. Each mark carries with a time allocation of 1.8 minutes (including time for selecting and reading questions). A 25 mark question therefore should be completed in 45 minutes.

- Once you have completed all of the questions in the body of this Practice & Revision Kit, you should attempt the **MOCK EXAMS** under examination conditions. Check your answers against our suggested solutions and marking scheme to find out how well you did.

This approach is only a suggestion. You or your college may well adapt it to suit your needs.

(vi)

SYLLABUS

Preparing Taxation Computations (GBR)

AIMS

To develop the ability to prepare computations of tax liability for both individuals and businesses resident in the UK for the purposes of income tax, corporation tax, capital gains tax and value added tax. In addition, to develop knowledge and understanding of the manner in which dealings must be conducted with HM Revenue and Customs, including knowledge of the statutory timescales for the submission of claims and returns and the due dates for the payment of tax liabilities.

OBJECTIVES

On completion of this paper, candidates should be able to:

- prepare adjusted profit / loss computations for trades and professions
- calculate an individual's income from employment
- prepare computations of property and investment income
- prepare income tax computations
- prepare computations of the chargeable gains arising on disposals by both individuals and companies
- prepare corporation tax computations
- complete and submit value added tax calculations using data from the appropriate recording systems
- identify the due dates for submission of returns and the payment of tax liabilities
- conduct dealings with the HM Revenue & Customs and with clients in an appropriate manner.

POSITION OF THE PAPER IN THE OVERALL SYLLABUS

An understanding of the format of accounts used for sole traders, partnerships and companies is assumed from Paper 3, *Maintaining Financial Records* and Paper 6, *Drafting Financial Statements*, but no prior knowledge of taxation is required.

SYLLABUS CONTENT

1   **Adjusted profit / loss computations for trades and professions**
   (a)   Adjustment of trading profits / losses for tax purposes
   (b)   Capital allowances
        (i)   definition of plant
        (ii)   allowances on plant and machinery
        (iii) private use assets
        (iv)   short life assets
        (v)   hire purchase and leasing
        (vi)   industrial buildings
   (c)   Assessments
        (i)   basis of assessment
        (ii)   sole traders and partnerships
   (d)   Relief for losses

2   **National insurance contributions**
   (a)   Class 2 and Class 4 National Insurance Contributions for the self employed
   (b)   Class 1 and 1A National Insurance Contributions for employees and employers

3   **Income from employment**
   (a)   Computing taxable earnings from employment
        (i)   basis of assessment
        (ii)   employment or self-employment
   (b)   Allowable deductions
   (c)   Benefits
   (d)   (i)   contributions to occupational pension schemes
        (ii)   charitable giving through the payroll

4   **Property and investment income**
   (a)   Profits / losses from property income
        (i)   computation of property income profits / losses
        (ii)   furnished holiday lettings
        (iii) rent a room scheme
        (iv)   relief for property income losses
   (b)   Other investments
        (i)   bank, building society and other interest
        (ii)   dividends
        (iii) tax exempt investments

5   **Income tax computations**
   (a)   Computing taxable income
        (i)   the aggregation of income
        (ii)   charges on income
        (iii) the personal allowance for individuals under 65
   (b)   Computing income tax payable
        (i)   allocation of tax rates / bands to savings income, non-savings income and dividend income

Preparing Taxation Computations (GBR)

(ii) relief for:
  – charitable donations
  – personal pension contributions

6 **Chargeable gain computations (individuals and companies)**
  (a) Chargeable persons, disposals and assets
  (b) Computing gains and losses
    (i) the basic computation
    (ii) valuing assets
    (iii) indexation allowance
    (iv) part disposals
    (v) taper relief for individuals
  (c) Share and securities
    (i) matching rules for individuals
    (ii) matching rules for companies
    (iii) FA 1985 pool
    (iv) bonus and rights issues
    (v) gilts and qualifying corporate bonds
  (d) Other areas of capital gains tax (including reliefs)
    (i) gift relief
    (ii) rollover relief
    (iii) principal private residence relief
    (iv) chattels
    (v) relief for losses
    (vi) compensation and insurance proceeds
  (e) Computing capital gains tax payable

7 **Administration of income tax and capital gains tax**
  (a) Self-assessment system
  (b) Payment of income tax (including payments on account) and capital gains tax
  (c) Enquiries
  (d) Dealing with the Inland Revenue and client confidentiality

8 **Corporation tax computations**
  (a) Company profits chargeable to corporation tax
  (b) Accounting periods
  (c) Computing corporation tax
  (d) Relief for losses (trade and non-trade)

9 **Administration of corporation tax**
  (a) Corporation tax self-assessment
  (b) The payment of corporation tax (including quarterly payments on account)
  (c) Dealing with the Inland Revenue and client confidentiality

10 **Value added tax (VAT)**
  (a) Scope of VAT
  (b) Basic principles of VAT
    (i) types of supply
    (ii) computing VAT due
    (iii) accounting for VAT
    (iv) the time of supply
  (c) VAT invoices and records
  (d) Registration
  (e) Administration of VAT

EXCLUDED TOPICS

The following topics are specifically excluded from Paper 9:

Adjusted profit computations for trades and professions:
- badges of trade
- successions
- change of accounting date
- long life assets
- capital allowances on agricultural buildings, hotels and intangible assets
- in respect of industrial buildings allowances: enterprise zones, initial allowances and the sale of industrial buildings following a period of non-industrial use
- notional profits / losses for partnerships
- limited liability partnerships
- personal service companies
- the special rules for losses in the opening years of a trade (s. 381 ICTA 1988)
- the special rules for losses in the closing years of a trade (terminal losses under s. 388 ICTA 1988)
- the special rules for the use of trade losses against capital gains (s. 72 FA 1991).

Preparing Taxation Computations (GBR)

Income from employment:

- detailed operation of the PAYE system (including calculations of code numbers)
- share incentive schemes
- termination payments.

Property and investment income:

- the enterprise investment scheme and venture capital trusts
- trust income.

Income tax computations:

- personal allowances other than the personal allowance for people aged under 65
- tax reducers
- foreign income and double tax relief.

Chargeable gains:

- calculation of the indexation allowance for individuals
- reinvestment relief
- assets held at 31 March 1982
- negligible value claims
- substantial shareholdings
- wasting assets (other than chattels) and leases
- connected persons and transfers between spouses
- incorporation relief
- damaged assets.

Corporation tax:

- close companies
- non-trading deficits on loan relationships
- relief for intangible assets
- the corporate venturing scheme
- groups and consortia
- foreign income and double tax relief
- investment companies and companies in receivership / liquidation
- completion of forms CT61.

Value added tax:

- group registration
- secondhand goods scheme

- partial exemption
- special schemes for retailers
- the capital goods scheme
- serious misdeclaration penalty
- default interest.

National insurance contributions:

- for Class 4: the offset of trading losses against non-trading income
- contracted out contributions.

KEY AREAS OF THE SYLLABUS

The key topic areas are as follows:

- computation of adjusted profits / losses for trades and professions
- calculating an individual's income from employment
- assessment of profits / losses from trades or professions
- basic income tax computations
- basic chargeable gains computations
- computing profits chargeable to corporation tax
- computing corporation tax payable
- income tax and corporation tax self assessment
- basic value added tax computations.

STUDY SESSIONS

Preparing Taxation Computations (GBR)

STUDY SESSIONS

1   **Introduction to the UK tax system**

(a)   Identify the main sources of UK tax legislation

(b)   Identify the key reference sources for UK tax legislation

(c)   Describe the organisation HM Revenue & Customs and its terms of reference including the appeals system

(d)   Describe the appeals process for income tax special and general commissioners

(e)   Explain the system of income tax and its background (how the legislation does not define income but defines taxable sources)

2   **Introduction to personal taxation**

(a)   Identify the fiscal year

(b)   Outline the scope of income tax: chargeable persons, chargeable income

(c)   Distinguish between income and capital profits/losses

(d)   Outline the key elements of a personal income tax computation

(i)   earned income

(ii)   non-savings income

(iii)   savings income

(iv)   dividend income

(v)   statutory total income

(vi)   taxable income

3   **Income from savings and investments**

(a)   Identify investments taxed at source

(b)   Identify tax-free investments

(c)   Identify the source documents used to complete the tax return

(d)   Prepare schedules of savings income to accompany the tax return

4   **Income tax – assessments**

(a)   Explain the entitlement to and the amount of the personal allowance

(b)   Identify and explain the use of charges on income

(i)   eligible interest

(ii)   patent and copyright royalties

(c)   Illustrate the allocation of tax bands and tax rates

against statutory total income (STI)

(i)   non-savings

(ii)   savings

(iii)   dividends

(d)   Explain and illustrate the difference between tax liability and tax payable for:

(i)   deduction of tax credits from savings and dividend income

(ii)   deduction of PAYE

(e)   Explain and illustrate charitable payments

(i)   payroll giving

(ii)   gift aid and the extension of basic rate band

(f)   Prepare examples of income tax computations

(i)   standard layout

(ii)   statutory total income (STI)

(iii)   use of rates and bands

(iv)   basic rate band extension

(v)   tax liability and tax payable

5   **Income tax – employment income I**

(a)   Explain the difference between employment and self-employment

(b)   Identify assessable income

(i)   salaries

(ii)   commissions

(iii)   bonuses

(iv)   benefits

(c)   Define and illustrate the basis of assessment for:

(i)   directors

(ii)   others

(d)   Identify the principal categories of deductions and illustrate their scope (no detail on pension contributions at this point)

(i)   payroll giving

(ii)   subscriptions

(iii)   travelling expenses

(iv)   expenses incurred wholly, exclusively and necessarily in the performance of duties

Preparing Taxation Computations (GBR)

6   Income tax – employment income 2

(a)   Define and distinguish between higher and lower paid employees

(b)   Identify the information required on a P11D and a P9D

(c)   Identify and calculate benefits

    (i)   assessable on all employees

    (ii)   assessable on the lower paid

    (iii)   assessable on the higher paid

(d)   Identify the circumstances when a general business expenses dispensation may be available, how it works and its implications on the employer and employee

7   Income tax – employment income 3

(a)   Compute aggregate income

    (i)   all income

    (ii)   benefits

    (iii)   expenses

(b)   Identify source documents required to complete tax returns

    (i)   interest statements

    (ii)   receipts for expenses

    (iii)   Forms P11D or P9D

    (iv)   Form P60

(c)   Compute basic Class 1 National Insurance Contributions

    (i)   employees

    (ii)   employers (including class 1A)

8   Income tax – income from trade and professions 1

(a)   Explain the principles of deductible and non-deductible expenditure

(b)   Prepare adjusted profit computations (pre capital allowances)

9   Income tax – income from trade and professions 2

(a)   Explain the basis of assessment for a continuing sole trader's business

(b)   Explain and demonstrate the calculations of the basis of assessment for commencement and cessation of businesses

(c)   Calculate overlap relief, explain and demonstrate how it can be used on cessation

10   Capital allowances 1

(a)   Explain the principles relating to capital allowances on plant and machinery

    (i)   definition of plant

    (ii)   cars

    (iii)   private use assets

    (iv)   short life assets

    (v)   hire purchase and leasing

(b)   Prepare capital allowance computations for plant and machinery

    (i)   writing down allowance

    (ii)   first year allowance

    (iii)   restrictions

11   Capital allowances 2

(a)   Explain the principles relating to capital allowances on industrial buildings

    (i)   qualifying trades

    (ii)   qualifying expenditure

    (iii)   qualifying industrial use

(b)   Explain non–industrial use and notional allowances

(c)   Prepare capital allowance calculations for industrial buildings

    (i)   new buildings

    (ii)   second-hand buildings

    (iii)   disposals

12   Income from trade and professions 3

(a)   Prepare adjusted profit calculations (including capital allowances)

(b)   Illustrate the use of capital allowances at the commencement and cession of businesses

(c)   Calculate National Insurance Contributions for the self-employed and contrast with employees

    (i)   class 2

    (ii)   class 4

Preparing Taxation Computations (GBR)

13   Income from trade and professions 4

(a)   Explain the alternative loss reliefs available to a sole trader

(i)   s.380 current and prior years

(ii)   s.385 carried forward

(b)   Demonstrate the best use of a loss relief claim

(i)   save the highest amount of tax

(ii)   timing

(iii)   protection of personal allowances

14   Partnerships

(a)   Explain how the trading profit rules are adapted for partnerships

(b)   Explain and show the effect of capital allowances on partnerships

(c)   Demonstrate the effect of changes in partnerships

(i)   change in profit sharing ratios

(ii)   new partners

(iii)   departing partners

(d)   Illustrate the loss relief claims available to individual partners

15   Income from property – individuals

(a)   Identify property income assessable

(i)   furnished and unfurnished property

(ii)   premiums from short leases

(b)   Outline the deductions allowable

(i)   revenue expenses

(ii)   capital allowances

(iii)   wear and tear allowance

(iv)   repairs and renewals

(v)   restriction for private use

(c)   Rent a room relief

(d)   Furnished holiday lettings

(e)   Use of losses

16   Pension contributions

(a)   Identify the schemes available

(i)   occupational pension schemes

(ii)   private pension plans

(b)   Define net relevant earnings

(c)   Explain the maximum contributions allowed for tax relief

(i)   occupational schemes

(ii)   personal pension plans

(iii)   stakeholder plans

(iv)   employee, employer and self employed

(d)   Show how the relief is given

(i)   deductions from salary

(ii)   basic rate tax withheld at source

(iii)   higher rate tax relief given via basic rate band extension

(e)   Explain the principles of relating back private pension plan premiums to the previous year

(f)   Show the tax effects of employer contributions

(i)   on the employer

(ii)   on the employee

17   Income tax administration

(a)   Self assessment forms

(i)   requirement

(ii)   completion dates

(b)   Pay As You Earn (PAYE) forms and deadlines for submission

(i)   P11D

(ii)   P9D

(iii)   P14

(iv)   P60

(v)   P35

(vi)   P45

(c)   Payment dates

(i)   employees

(ii)   self employed

18   Capital gains tax – basic principles

(a)   Define chargeable persons, chargeable disposals and chargeable assets

(i)   individuals and companies

(ii)   exempt disposals

(iii)   exempt assets

(b)   Outline the administrative framework for capital gains tax

(i)   individuals

(iii)   payment

(c)   Outline the use of tax bands and rates in conjunction

Preparing Taxation Computations (GBR)

with income tax

(d)   Outline the basic calculation including the deduction of expenses of purchase and sale

(e)   Explain the entitlement to the annual exemption

19   **Capital gains tax – basic computations**

(a)   Explain the circumstances when market value may be used for the transfer value

 (i)   bargains not at arms length

 (ii)   gifts

(b)   Demonstrate the calculation of market value for quoted shares and securities

(c)   Explain the indexation allowance for individuals as applied in the period March 1982 to April 1998 (Note: Calculation of this will not be required in the examination as the indexed value at April 1998 will be given)

(d)   Explain and calculate taper relief for individuals

 (i)   business assets

 (ii)   non-business assets

(e)   Explain the differences for companies

 (i)   calculate indexation allowance up to the date of sale

 (ii)   no taper relief

(f)   Calculate disposals of post 31 March 1982 assets

 (i)   include enhancement expenditure

 (ii)   purchases pre and post April 1998

(g)   Explain the use of capital losses

 (i)   current year

 (ii)   brought forward

20   **Capital gains tax – shares and securities I**

(a)   Outline the matching rules for individuals

 (i)   same day

 (ii)   next 30 days

 (iii)   since April 1998

 (iv)   FA 1985 Pool (indexed value at April 1998 will be given)

(b)   Compute gains and losses on disposals by individuals

(c)   Outline the matching rules for companies

 (i)   same day

 (ii)   last 9 days

 (iii)   FA 1985 pool (construction of a basic pool, including the calculation of indexation allowance up to the date of sale will be required)

(d)   Compute gains and losses on disposals by companies

21   **Capital gains tax – shares and securities 2**

(a)   Illustrate the impact of bonus and rights issues on shareholdings

(b)   Sale of rights – awareness of basic treatment (partial vs.small disposal) only

(c)   Identify exempt disposals

 (i)   gilts

 (ii)   qualifying corporate bonds (individuals only)

22   **Capital gains tax – chattels, part disposals, compensation and insurance**

(a)   Define chattels

 (i)   non-wasting

 (ii)   wasting

(b)   Explain and demonstrate the calculation of gains on chattel disposals

 (i)   exemptions

 (ii)   marginal relief

 (iii)   deemed proceeds for losses

 (iv)   awareness of the interaction with capital allowances

(c)   Calculate gains on part disposals

(d)   Compensation and insurance proceeds

23   **Capital gains tax – further reliefs**

(a)   Outline the rules governing principal private residence (PPR)

 (i)   exemption

 (ii)   relief for absences

 (iii)   letting relief

(b)   Gift Relief

 (i)   outline availability

 (ii)   explain and calculate the relief

 (iii)   calculate the restriction as a result of a sale at undervalue

Preparing Taxation Computations (GBR)

(c)   Roll-over relief

(i)   outline availability

(ii)   explain and calculate the relief

(iii)   calculate the relief available on the partial reinvestment of sale proceeds and/or partial business use of an asset

(iv)   explain the consequences of reinvestment in depreciating or non-depreciating assets

24   Corporation tax – compute the profits liable to corporation tax

(a)   Identify the scope of corporation tax

(i)   chargeable entities

(ii)   chargeable income

(b)   Identify chargeable accounting periods

(c)   Identify the basis of assessment for all sources of income

(i)   Trading income

(ii)   Profits from loan relationships and interest

(iii)   Property business income

(iv)   capital gains

(d)   Compute profits chargeable to corporation tax (PCTCT)

25   Corporation tax – computation of tax liability

(a)   Identify the financial year(s) relevant to a chargeable accounting period

(b)   Identify the rates of corporation tax to be applied

(i)   starting rate

(ii)   lower marginal rate

(iii)   small companies rate

(iv)   higher marginal rate

(v)   full rate

(c)   Calculate the corporation tax liability

(d)   Calculate the minimum amount of tax payable by small companies

(e)   Calculate and offset any income tax on payments and receipt

(f)   Identify associate companies and show their effect on tax calculations

26   Corporation tax – other aspects

(a)   Calculate the corporation tax payable for periods longer and shorter than 12 months

(b)   Explain the loss reliefs available for both trade and non trade losses

(c)   Illustrate the use of the loss reliefs in a basic calculation

(i)   trade losses

–   s393A (1) current period

–   s393A (1) carry back (including cessation)

–   s395 carry forward

(ii)   non trade losses

–   Property business loss relief

–   capital losses

–   explain the impact of cessation of trade on trade and non trade losses

(d)   Compute corporation tax repayable following a loss relief claim

27   Corporation tax – administration

(a)   Outline the corporation tax self assessment rules

(i)   return and filing date

(ii)   amendments and enquiries

(b)   Illustrate and calculate methods of payment of tax

(i)   small and medium size companies

(ii)   large companies

28   Value Added Tax (VAT)

(a)   Explain the scope of VAT

(b)   Illustrate the need for registration

(i)   compulsory

(ii)   voluntary

(iii)   exemption

(iv)   deregistration

(c)   Explain and contrast the types of supply

(i)   standard

(ii)   zero rated

(iii)   exempt

(d)   Compute VAT liability

(i)   input tax

(ii)   output tax

(iii)   bad debts

(iv)   discounts

(v)   irrecoverable VAT

(e)   Account for VAT

Preparing Taxation Computations (GBR)

(i)   return periods

(ii)   tax point

(iii)   VAT return

(f)   Explain the detail required on VAT invoices

(g)   Detail the basic VAT administration requirements

(i)   records

(ii)   late registration penalties

(h)   Explain the treatment of imports and exports

(i)   Describe the following schemes

(i)   annual accounting scheme

(ii)   cash accounting scheme

(iii)   flat rate scheme

29   **Revision of income tax**

30   **Revision of capital gains tax**

31   **Revision of corporation tax**

32   **Revision of VAT**

APPROACH TO EXAMINING THE SYLLABUS

Assessment methods and format of the paper

Paper 9 is a three-hour written paper. The examination will be predominantly computational.

Number of marks

Four compulsory questions   100

Question 1 will always relate to income tax for a minimum of 30 and no more than 35 marks.

Questions 2 and 3 will relate to corporation tax and capital gains tax respectively.

Question 4 may include topics from any area of syllabus not examined elsewhere in the paper.

Value added tax (VAT) will not be examined as a full question but will be examined as part of any of the questions involving a business, either linked to the business scenario contained in the remainder of the question or as a distinct and separate scenario.

Tax rates and allowances will be provided at the front of the paper.

Section numbers

Knowledge of section numbers will not be needed to understand questions in this paper, nor will students be expected to use them in their answers. If they wish to refer to section numbers in their answer they may do so and will not be penalised if old, or even incorrect section numbers are used.

Analysis of past questions

June and December 2005 papers

The June and December 2005 papers form the mock exams at the end of this Kit, so they are not analysed here.

December 2004

1   Income tax payable. NICs for employee. Taxable benefits. Personal Pensions.

2   Company with long period of account. Capital allowances. CT calculation. VAT compulsory registration.

3   Gains for individuals: part disposal, house, shares. Gift relief.

4   Partnership income tax. Industrial buildings allowance.

What the examiner said

'The examination consisted of four compulsory questions each being split in sub parts. The questions were based on the usual theme of firstly income tax, then corporation tax followed by capital gains tax with the last on any other part of the syllabus, which in this instance was partnerships and industrial buildings allowance.

Most candidates attempted all question but many left out some sub parts with VAT and capital gains tax relief being the most frequently omitted.

Workings were generally shown but were at times difficult to follow. Too many candidates continue to display their answers poorly, with a lack of clear labelling to indicate which questions are being attempted. Each question should be started on a new page and candidates must give

(xvi)

more thought to the layout and organisation of their answers. Where a question asks for a particular format, for example question 2(a) – a letter to a client – then this must be done to earn the presentation marks available.

As is becoming the usual trend many candidates were well prepared for the income tax question but, in some cases, found the corporation tax and capital tax areas a complete mystery! Several candidates are failing this paper because they seem to be concentrating on income tax only – scoring well on question 1 – and then scoring very little on the rest of the paper. Once again candidates are reminded that they must study the entire syllabus if they want to be successful!'

June 2004

1   Income tax payable. PAYE forms. Self assessment. NICs for employers and employees. Property business income.

2   Capital allowances (P&M, IBAs) for company. CT payable. VAT return calculation.

3   CGT for individuals: chattel, shares, painting. Rollover relief for business assets.

4   Capital allowances for sole trader. Basis of assessment of trading profit.

What the examiner said

This was the first paper under the revised syllabus and most answers showed that candidates had prepared well for this paper.

It consisted of four compulsory Questions, broken into sub parts giving a wide coverage of syllabus topics. Question 1 was on income tax and as usual provided to be the most popular area of the paper. The other three Questions were on corporation tax, capital gains tax and sole trader profit assessment. These Questions produced varying standards of answers with the capital gains tax Question proving the most difficult.

Value Added Tax (VAT) has been included in the syllabus for the first time and many candidates seemed to be well prepared for this new topic. However many had obviously never heard of VAT and made little attempt at this part of Question 2. VAT will appear in all examinations in the future.

The other new area to the syllabus is 'communication skills' which, in this paper, required a simple letter to a client. Many candidates were aware of the need to answer in a letter format and gained simple marks for a basic layout. Again this new area will appear in all future examinations in one of the four Questions.

It was pleasing to see the vast improvement in the layout of candidates' answers with most now showing clear workings.

Pilot paper

1   Computation of income tax payable. Letter advising of due dates/penalties under self assessment.

2   Computation of CT payable. Computation of VAT repayment due.

3   Computation of CGT due/payment dates. Chattels, part disposal, gift relief.

4   Partnerships. Capital allowances/IBAs. Assessment in opening year.

Questions and answers

1   QUESTION WITH HELP: JULIE

In 2005/06, Julie has the following income.

	£
Salary (amount before tax)	39,000
Building society interest (amount received - net of 20% tax)	1,600
Lotto winnings	250

How much tax is due in total? If £7,500 of tax was deducted from her salary under PAYE, how much more tax must she pay?

> *If you are stuck, look at the next page for detailed help as to how you should tackle this question.*

APPROACHING THE ANSWER

Step 1   Set up a proforma computation

Step 2   Fill in the figures provided in the question, remembering to gross up the building society interest and exclude any exempt income

Step 3   Calculate taxable income

Step 4   Apply the bands to the taxable income to calculate income tax

Step 5   Deduct PAYE and income suffered at source

Step 6   Calculate the outstanding tax liability

1   ANSWER TO QUESTION WITH HELP: JULIE

	Non-savings £	Savings (excl dividends) £	Dividends £	Total £
Earnings	39,000		0	
Building society interest £1,600 × 100/80		2,000	0	
Statutory total income	39,000	2,000	0	41,000
Less personal allowance	(4,895)	0	0	(4,895)
Taxable income	34,105	2,000	0	36,105

Income tax

	£	£
£		
2,090 × 10%		209
30,310 × 22%		6,668
3,705 × 40%		1,482
36,105		
Income tax liability		8,359
Less: tax deducted under PAYE	7,500	
tax suffered on building society interest £2,000 × 20%	400	
		(7,900)
Balance of tax still to pay		459

Note. **Lotto winnings are exempt from tax**

2   BILL WILSON

Bill Wilson was employed as a works manager in a large UK resident company. He was made redundant on 1 January 2006.

During the year 2005/06 he had the following income.

	£	
Salary	34,747	(to 31 December 2005)
Dividends	1,350	(from UK companies) 1500.00
	1,600	(from ISA investments)
Interest	648	(from UK building societies) 910.00
	240	(from ISA)
Premium Bond Prize	50	

All the dividends and interest receipts are stated at the actual amounts received. The salary is stated at its gross amount.

During his employment he was provided with a petrol engined BMW car which had a list price of £20,000. The CO_2 emissions of the car were 177 g/km. The company paid for all of the petrol.   *3300* *3168*

Bill had made a payment during 2005/06 of £400 (gross) to a registered charity under the Gift Aid scheme.

Required

(a) Calculate Bill's income tax payable (prior to PAYE deductions) for the tax year 2005/06.   (13 marks)

(b) Give reasons where you have left any amounts out of the calculations.   (3 marks)

(c) List FIVE types of expenses that Bill could deduct from his earnings.   (5 marks)

(d) Explain the PAYE procedures required in relation to Bill's termination of employment.   (6 marks)

(27 marks)

Helping hand

This is a typical income tax computation. Set up your pro forma with headings for non-savings income, savings and dividends. Be careful where benefits are only received for part of the year.

Allocate your time carefully between each part of the question. You are more likely to pass the question if you have made some attempt at each part, than if you have just answered one part perfectly.

7

2   **ANSWER: BILL WILSON**

> **Helping hand**
>
> Here benefits have only been received for 9 months out of 12 months so need to be reduced appropriately.

(a)   **Bill Wilson – Income tax payable 2005/06**

	Non-savings income £	Savings (excl. dividends) income £	Dividend income £	Total income £
Salary	34,747			
Car benefit (W2)	3,300			
Fuel benefit (W3)	2,376			
Dividends £1,350 × 100/90			1,500	
Interest £648 × 100/80		810		
STI	40,423	810	1,500	42,733
Less: PA	(4,895)			(4,895)
Taxable income	35,528	810	1,500	37,838

Tax

	£
Non-savings income	
£2,090 × 10%	209
£30,310 × 22%	6,668
£400 × 22% (Gift Aid)	88
£(35,528 − 32,400 − 400) = £2,728 × 40%	1,091
Savings (excluding dividends) income	
£810 × 40%	324
Dividend income	
£1,500 × 32.5%	487
	8,867
Tax liability	
Less: tax on dividends £1,500 × 10%	(150)
tax on BSI interest £810 × 20%	(162)
Tax payable (before PAYE)	8,555

Workings

1   *Taxable car %*

CO2 emissions above baseline

175 g/km − 140 g/km = 35 g/km (round down)

Divide by 5 = 35/5 = 7

% = 15% + 7% = 22%

2   *Car benefit*

22% (W1) × £20,000 × 9/12 =   £3,300

3   *Fuel benefit*

22% (W1) × £14,400 × 9/12 =   £2,376

(b) **Amounts left out of calculation**

 (i) Dividends from ISA investments – not taxable.

 (ii) Interest from ISA – not taxable.

 (iii) Premium Bond Prize – not taxable.

(c) **Five expenses deductible from earnings**

Any five from:

 (i) Contributions (within certain limits) to an approved occupational pension scheme

 (ii) Subscriptions to professional bodies if relevant to occupation

 (iii) Payments for certain liabilities relating to employment and insurance against them

 (iv) Payments under the payroll deduction scheme

 (v) Authorised mileage allowance relief

 (vi) Qualifying travel expenses

 (vii) Other expenses incurred wholly, exclusively and necessarily in the performance of the duties of the employment

 (viii) Capital allowances on plant and machinery (other than cars or other vehicles) necessarily provided for use in the performance of those duties

(d) **PAYE procedures on termination of employment**

When an employee leaves employment, **the employer must prepare a form P45** (Particulars of Employee Leaving).

The form shows the employee's code and details of his income and tax paid to date.

The form is in four parts. **One part is sent to HMRC and three parts given to the employee**

One of the parts (part 1A) is the **employee's personal cop**y.

If the employee takes up new employment, he hands the remaining two parts to his new employer.

The **new employer** fills in details of the new employment, keeps one copy (to use for calculating tax on the new employment) **and sends the other copy to HMRC.**

Marking guide

		Marks	
(a)	Car benefit	3	
	Fuel	2	
	Dividends	1	
	Interest	1	
	PA	1	
	Gift Aid extension to BRB	1	
	Calculation of tax	3	
	Tax credits	1	13
(b)	Left out of calculations – one mark each		3
(c)	Five expenses – one mark each		5
(d)	P45 needed	1	
	Details	1	
	4 parts	1	
	Part 1A	1	
	2 parts to new employer	1	
	New employer procedure	1	6
			27

What the examiner said

'This included, as always, a standard personal tax computation. The problem posed in this question was whether the interest and dividends received were taxable or not and, if so how much. Many candidates were not aware that dividends and interest from ISAs were tax-free.

It was surprising to find that although this is a standard question, many candidates were not aware of the very basic layout required for this type of computation.

The theory parts of the question asked for a basic knowledge of expenses and PAYE rules. These areas were poorly answered. Expenses must not be confused with charges on income and payments towards benefits – what was required were payments wholly, exclusively and necessarily incurred in the performance of duty.

PAYE rules should be known as basic knowledge expected of a taxation technician.'

3   **JASON ROBERTS**

Jason Roberts is married to Kathy.

Jason works part-time and has the following income for the tax year 2005/06:

	£
Salary	16,461
UK Dividends – amount of cash received	460
Bank Deposit Interest – amount credited to his account	2,400

He paid £312 (net) to a national charity under the gift aid rules.

Kathy is employed as a sales representative and has an annual salary of £26,545. She contributes 5% of her gross salary to an occupational pension scheme.

Kathy uses her own car for all business journeys and claims the company's standard mileage allowance of 20.5p per mile. Total business miles travelled, and claimed for, amounted to 7,000 in 2005/06. Kathy always claims any expense entitlement against her earnings.

Kathy had an interest free loan from her employer obtained to help purchase a yacht. The average amount outstanding for the year 2005/06 amounted to £12,000.

Jason and Kathy own their own house and have a lodger who pays them £4,940 per year. The income is shared equally between them.

In addition to the above Kathy also received in 2005/06:

	£
Building Society interest – amount credited to her account	684
Interest on ISA – amount credited to account	480

On 15 March 2006 Kathy inherited an antique desk from her uncle. This had cost Kathy's uncle £2,000 in June 2004 and had a value of £8,800 when inherited by Kathy. It was not a business asset. Kathy plans to sell the desk in November 2006 and hopes to receive £19,000 because an interested dealer had discovered a matching chair.

Required

(a)   Calculate the income tax liabilities for the tax year 2005/06 for:

    (i)   Mr Roberts   (12 marks)

    (ii)   Mrs Roberts   (13 marks)

(b)   Explain the capital gains tax (CGT) implications of:

    (i)   The inheritance of the desk, and

    (ii)   The proposed sale of the desk

    Note: You are not required to work out the actual CGT payable   (5 marks)

Assume the official rate of interest is 5%.   **(30 marks)**

3   ANSWER: JASON ROBERTS

(a)   (i)   **Mr Roberts income tax 2005/06**

	Non savings Income £	Savings Income £	Dividend Income £	Total Income £
Salary	16,461			
Rental income (N)	345			
Bank interest £2,400 × $\frac{100}{80}$		3,000		
Dividends £460 × $\frac{100}{90}$			511	
STI	16,806	3,000	511	20,317
Less: PA	(4,895)			(4,895)
Taxable income	11,911	3,000	511	15,422

Note: rental income of £4,940 ÷ 2 = £2,470, partly covered by 'rent-a-room' exemption of £4,250 ÷ 2 = £2,125.

Elect by 31.01.08 for this treatment.

Tax

	£
£2,090 @ 10%	209
£(11,911 – 2,090) = £9,821 @ 22%	2,161
£3,000 @ 20%	600
£511 @ 10%	51
Income tax	3,021
Less: tax on bank interest	(600)
dividend credits	(51)
Income tax payable	2,370

Note: No further relief is given for the Gift Aid payment as it is treated as having been paid net of basic rate tax. If Jason Roberts had been a higher rate taxpayer the basic rate band would have been extended to give him additional rate tax relief on the gift aid donation.

(ii)   **Mrs Roberts income tax 2005/06**

	Non savings Income £	Savings Income £	Total Income £
Salary	26,545		
Less: pension 5%	(1,327)		
	25,218		
Less: mileage allowance (W1)	(1,365)		
	23,853		
Benefit (W2)	600	24,453	
Rental (see above)		345	
BSI £684 × $\frac{100}{80}$		855	
STI	24,798	855	25,653
Less: PA	(4,895)		(4,895)
Taxable income	19,903	855	20,758

Note: Interest from ISA is tax free.

Workings

			£
1	Statutory mileage rates		
	7,000 miles @ 40p		2,800
	Less: allowed by company		
	7,000 @ 20.5p		(1,435)
	Allowance		1,365

2	Loan benefit		
	£12,000 × 5%		£600

Tax

	£
£2,090 @ 10%	209
£(19,903 – 2,090) = £17,813 @ 22%	3,919
£855 @ 20%	171
Income tax	4,299
Less: tax on building society interest	(75)
Income tax payable	4,224

(b) (i) There was no disposal of the desk by Kathy's uncle on his death. Kathy is deemed to acquire the asset on 15 March 2006. However, Kathy's base cost is £8,800. Therefore the gain of Kathy's uncle is "washed out".

(ii) When Kathy sells the desk her gain will be:

	£
Proceeds	19,000
Less: cost	(8,800)
Gain	10,200

There will be no taper relief as Kathy has not owned the desk for 3 years.

The annual exemption of £8,500 will reduce the gain to £1,700.

Marking guide				Marks	
(a)	(i)	Salary		1	
		Rental income (including explanations)		3	
		BI		1	
		Dividends		1	
		PA		1	
		Tax calculation		3	
		Treatment of gift aid donation		2	12
	(ii)	Salary		1	
		Pension deduction		1	
		Mileage allowance		2	
		Benefit		2	
		Rental income		1	
		BSI		1	
		ISA interest		1	
		PA		1	
		Tax calculation		3	13
(b)	(i)	Desk – description		2	
	(ii)	Gain on disposal		3	
					5
					30

4   TONY GRAY (12/04)

(a)   Tony Gray is 43 years old and is employed as an advertising manager for Ads4U Ltd, a UK resident company.

It is now 14 June 2006 and Tony is preparing his tax return for the tax year 2005/06. He has gathered together the following documents and other information for that year.

- Form P60 showing taxable employment income of £39,610 and tax deducted of £7,272

- Form P11D showing total taxable benefits received of £2,290

- A bank statement from County Bank plc showing net interest credited of £280

- An interest statement from Town Building Society showing net interest credited of £360

- A statement from City Building Society showing interest credited of £120 from an individual savings account (ISA)

- Dividend vouchers showing cash dividends received totalling £270

- A letting agent's statement showing taxable property business income of £820

- An amount of £312 was paid to a registered charity under the gift aid scheme

Required

(i)   Calculate Tony's income tax payable for the tax year 2005/06.   (11 marks)

(ii)   State the two ways in which HMRC may collect any tax owing for the tax year 2005/06.
                                                                                          (3 marks)

(iii)   Calculate Tony's total Class 1 national insurance contributions (NIC) for the tax year 2005/06.
                                                                                          (3 marks)

(iv)   Calculate the total employers Class 1 and Class 1A NIC paid by Ads4U Ltd in respect of Tony for the tax year 2005/06.
                                                                                          (3 marks)

(b)   Tony's wife Trudy is also employed by Ads4U Ltd earning in excess of £35,000 every year. During the tax year 2005/06 she received the following benefits:

- A 2000 cc commercial van first registered in August 2003, used privately for 40% of the time. This was made available for Trudy's use for the whole of 2005/06. Ads4U Ltd paid for all of the running costs including petrol, which amounted to £600 for the year.

- A home entertainment system. This was first provided for Trudy to use at home on 6 April 2003, the date it was purchased by her employer at a cost of £1,200. The system was given to Trudy to keep on 6 October 2005 when it was worth £300.

- An allowance of £14 per night to cover miscellaneous expenses for overseas business trips totalling 80 nights.

- Luncheon vouchers amounting to £336 in respect of 224 working days.

- A mileage allowance of 55p per mile for the 6,000 business miles travelled by Trudy in her own car.

Required

Calculate the total value of Trudy's taxable benefits for the year 2005/06.   (9 marks)

(c)   Trudy is 41 years old. She has never previously contributed to a personal pension plan, but feels it is now time to think about her retirement.

Her net relevant earnings (NRE) for the past 6 tax years have been:

2000/2001	£41,000
2001/2002	£43,000
2002/2003	£38,000
2003/2004	£42,000
2004/2005	£41,000
2005/2006	£42,000

It is now 20 September 2006.

Questions and answers

Required

Advise Trudy of:

(i) The maximum amount that she may pay into a private pension plan for the tax year 2005/06.
(2 marks)

(ii) The latest date by which the premium must be paid.
(1 mark)

(iii) How tax relief will be given for the contributions paid.
(2 marks)

(34 marks)

4   ANSWER: TONY GRAY

(a) **Tutorial Note.** There is a statutory benefit of £500 for private use of a commercial van (£350 if van is at least 4 years old at the end of the fiscal year). This includes ancillary benefits such as servicing, petrol.

Remember the excess over the exempt amount for luncheon vouchers (15p) and mileage allowance (40p) is taxable. Whereas if the limit for incidental overnight expenses of £5 for UK and £10 for overseas is exceeded it all becomes taxable.

(a) (i)   **Tony Gray – tax payable 2005/06**

	Non-savings income £	Savings (exc dividend) income £	Dividend income £	Total £
Salary	39,610			
Benefits	2,290			
Property business income	820			
Bank interest (£280 × 100/80)		350		
Building soc interest (£360 × 100/80)		450		
Dividend (£270 × 100/90)			300	
Statutory total income (STI)	42,720	800	300	43,820
Less: personal allowance	(4,895)			(4,895)
Taxable income	37,825	800	300	38,925

Interest on ISA is exempt.

	£	£
Tax on non savings income		
£2,090 × 10%	209	
£30,310 × 22%	6,668	
£400 (£312 × 100/78) × 22%	88	
£5,025 × 40%	2,010	
Tax on savings (exc dividend) income		
£800 × 40%	320	
Tax on dividend income		
£300 × 32.5%	97	
		9,392
Less: tax suffered		
Tax credit on dividend		(30)
Tax on interest (£70 + £90)		(160)
PAYE		(7,272)
Income tax payable		1,930

(ii)   HMRC can collect the tax owing for 2005/06 as follows.

(1) Full settlement on or before 31 January 2007. (*Note:* No payments on account required as 80% or more of the tax liability is settled through deductions at source such as PAYE, basic rate on interest.)

(2) As the tax owed for 2005/06 is less than £2,000 it can be collected by adjusting the 2007/08 PAYE code. The tax return must be received by the Revenue on or before 30 September 2006.

(iii) **Tony Gray – Class 1 NIC**

	£
(£32,760 – £4,895) × 11%	3,065
(£39,610 – £32,760) × 1%	68
	3,133

(iv) **Ads4U Ltd – NIC**

		£
Class 1 (£39,610 – £4,895) × 12.8%		4,444
Class 1A £2,290 × 12.8%		293 4,737

(b) **Trudy Gray**
 Benefits 2005/06

	£	£
Van (less than 4 yrs old) Note: petrol is included in the van benefit		500
Entertainment system – use 6 months only in 2005/06: 6/12 × £1,200 ×20%		120
Entertainment system – gift Original cost	1,200	
Less: benefit assessed already		
2003/04 (£1,200 × 20%)	(240)	
2004/05	(240)	
2005/06	(120) 600	
Current market value	300	
Higher of two		600
Overseas business trip expenses £10 exemption for each night spent has been exceeded		1,120
Meal vouchers 15p exemption for each working day £336 – (15p × 224 days)		302
Mileage allowance *Employer rate:* 55p × 6,000 miles	3,300	
Less: Authorised mileage rate 40p × 6,000 miles	(2,400)	900
Total benefits		3,542

(c) (i) **Trudy Gray**
 Maximum gross pension contribution 2005/06

Net Relevant Earnings	×	*Age Related %*
Highest of current fiscal year (2005/06) and 5 previous fiscal years (2000/2001 to 2004/05)		41 years at 6 April 05 20%

Choose £43,000 (2001/02)

Max contribution: £43,000 × 20% = £8,600

(ii) Pension premium for 2005/06 must be paid by 31 January 2007.

(iii) Private pension premiums are paid net of 22% tax.

Tax relief of 18% is given to higher rate (40%) taxpayers by extending the basic rate band by the gross contribution.

Marking guide

				Marks
(a)	(i)	Salary		½
		Benefits		½
		Property business income		½
		Bank interest		1
		Building society interest		1
		Dividend		1
		Personal allowance		½
		ISA interest is exempt		1
		Tax at 10%, 22%, 40%, 32.5%		2½
		Extend basic rate band		1
		Tax credit on dividend		½
		Tax credit on interest		½
		PAYE		½
	(ii)	31 January 2007		1
		2007/08 PAYE code		1
		Return submitted by 30 September 2006		1
	(iii)	at 11%		1½
		at 1%		1½
	(iv)	Salary		½
		Lower limit		½
		12.8%		½
		Benefits		1
		12.8%		½
				20
(b)		Van – statutory benefit		1
		Note: petrol included		½
		Entertainment system: use		1
		Entertainment system: gift		
		Original cost		½
		Benefit already assessed		1
		Current market value		½
		Higher of		½
		Overseas expenses		1½
		Luncheon vouchers		1
		Mileage allowance		1½
				9
(c)	(i)	NRE		1
		Age related %		1
	(ii)	31 January 2007		1
	(iii)	Net of 22%		1
		Extending basic rate band		1
				5
				34

What the examiner said

This was a three-part question broken down into different areas of income tax and national insurance. The question was deliberately set into sub parts to allow candidates to attempt the areas without the fear of lack of knowledge on one area having a knock on effect on the next area. This seemed to work for part (a) (i) of the question, which was a basic income tax assessment with many candidates scoring full marks. The only minor problems here were that ISA interest should have been omitted as being tax-free income and the basic rate band should have been extended by the gross payment under the gift aid scheme. Some candidates added the PAYE figure to the salary figure given, these and future candidates should note that any salary figure given will always be the gross amount on which any PAYE will be calculated.

Part (a) (ii) required candidates to state the ways in which HMRC collects outstanding tax. The simple answer should have been by payment in full by 31 January 2006 or by collection via the following years tax code where payment due is less than £2,000. Statements such as 'by cheque' or 'bank transfer' did not score marks!

Parts (a) (iii) and (iv) were on national insurance payments. It was pleasing to note that many candidates scored well in this area with only minor addition problems letting them down. However a few displayed a total misunderstanding for the employers' liability and calculated sums using class 2 and class 4 rules despite the question clearly asking for class 1 and class 1A. A few were unaware that class 1A was only paid by employers and then only on the benefits given.

Part (b) of the question was poorly answered with many displaying a total lack of knowledge on benefits. The question required the calculation of five different benefits however some calculated the tax due on Trudy's total income – no marks were available for this – candidates must read the requirement of any question carefully and only do that which is required.

Few candidates knew the rules for vans provided for private use. The benefit is a flat rate of £500 per year unless the van is more than four years old at the end of the year when the benefit is reduced to £350. The percentage of private use is irrelevant and the running costs including petrol are all covered by this flat rate. Many suggested that there wasn't enough information supplied and that CO_2 emissions should be given – this is not relevant for vans.

Some reasonable attempts at the value of the home entertainment system were made but in general many had no idea. Where private use of an asset is allowed without transfer of ownership then an annual benefit of 20% of cost is assessed on the employee. When ownership is subsequently transferred then in the year of transfer the employee is assessed on any use in the year at a pro rated annual benefit of 20% plus the higher of current market value and the tax written down value of the asset after the previous annual 20% benefits have been deducted from the original cost.

The overseas expense allowance is more straightforward. Few stated that the allowance is tax-free up to £10 per night but when this limit is exceeded then the full amount is assessable not just the amount above £10.

Most candidates knew the first 15p per day for meal vouchers is tax-free and only the excess above this is taxable.

Most candidates knew the mileage allowance rules but silly addition problems let some down. The taxable figure is the excess amount over 40p per mile (for the first 10,000 miles) paid to employees.

The final part of question 1 was on personal pension contributions. The amount allowed for tax relief is dependent on the age of the individual at the start of the year as given in the table of rates and allowances supplied and the highest net relevant earnings (NRE) in the current year or the previous five. Only about half of candidates were aware of this rule. The method of given tax relief was again only known by about half of the candidates sitting.'

5   MICKEY THOMAS (PILOT PAPER)

(a)   Mickey Thomas is aged 45 and is a senior employee of Johnson Brothers plc, a large UK resident manufacturing company based in the South of England. He is married with two children aged 12 and 13.

Mickey has the following income and expenditure for the tax year 2005/06.

Income from employment

A basic salary of £42,000 and annual bonuses of £4,000 paid in May 2005 and £5,000 paid in May 2006. These bonuses are paid annually in arrears based on the company's accounting periods to 30 April.

A company car, which was first provided by Johnson Brothers in 2004. It is a petrol driven 2000 cc BMW with CO2 emissions of 171g per kilometre. The car's list price was £24,000 but the company paid £23,500 inclusive of VAT. The company met all running costs in full.

The company also provided medical cover, which cost them £462 per employee, which is a saving of £96 per employee, were they to provide the same cover themselves.

A loan of £20,000 was advanced on 6 April 2005 at a rate of 1.5%. Mickey paid back £6,000 of the loan on 6 October 2005. The remaining £14,000 is still outstanding.

The company pays £50 per month to Mickey's private pension plan The plan was started in May 2004 and contributions have been made continuously since then.

The company has deducted income tax amounting to £11,180 in total under the PAYE system.

Other income

	£
Building society interest	480
Bank interest	596
UK dividend	270

All three figures are the cash amount received.

Expenditure

Contributions to his private pension plan   £200 (net) per month
(As above – started in May 2004).

Required

Calculate the income payable by Mickey for the tax year 2005/06.

(17 marks)

(b)   Charlie Bassett is a tax technician employed by 'Tax Help for You', a large UK resident partnership based in London.

On the morning of 23 September 2006 he received an e-mail from Peter Jones, an junior partner in the firm which contained the following message.

Hi Charlie

I received a letter from John Hunt yesterday. He is a new client and as part of your training I want you to take a look at the detail within the letter and draft an appropriate response for me to review.

A copy of his letter is attached.

Peter

Required

Using the information provided, draft a response to Mr Hunt, which supplies the information requested, and answers the specific questions posed in his letter.

The response must be in a suitable format and up to 2 marks will be awarded for its style and presentation.

(15 marks)

(32 marks)

LETTER FROM MR HUNT

John Hunt
22 The Street
Anywhere
England

16 September 2006

Peter Jones
'Tax Help for You'
16 The Road
London
England

Dear Peter

TAX ADVICE

I am employed as a general manager for Smith Brothers Ltd, based in Surrey. Up to now I have never had to complete a tax return before but recently I received a return from the Revenue, which I am not sure how to complete.

I have arranged, with your secretary, to meet with you on 2 October at 11.30 am.

I received and paid the following types of income and expenditure during the last tax year but I am not sure what information or documents you might require to complete the return.

Income

Salary (£32,000 approximately)
Loan of a company car
Private medical insurance provided by the company
Bank interest
Building Society interest
Interest from an Individual Savings Account

Payments

Contribution to a pension plan
Interest on a mortgage on my main residence
Subscription to the Institute of Personnel Managers

I would be grateful if you could inform me as to what I should bring with me to the meeting to help complete the tax return. Also could you answer the following questions?

(a)   When has the return to be returned to the Revenue?

(b)   When will the tax be paid and can I do it via my tax code?

(c)   Are there any penalties if the deadlines in (a) and (b) are not met, if so what are they?

(d)   My wife earns £6,500 a year – does this need to be included on my return?

Yours sincerely

John Hunt

24

5   **ANSWER: MICKEY THOMAS**

> **Helping hand.** The contributions made by the company to Mickey Thomas' private pension plan are not a taxable benefit for Mickey.
>
> Basic rate tax relief is given at source on the contributions that Mickey pays to the private pension plan. Additional relief is given by extending the basic rate band.

(a)

	Non-savings income £	Savings(excl dividend) income £	Dividend income £	Total £
Salary	42,000			
Bonus	4,000			
Car benefit (£24,000 × 21%) (W1)	5,040			
Fuel benefit (£14,400 × 21%) (W1)	3,024			
Medical cover	462			
Loan (W2)	595			
Bank interest		600		
Building society interest		745		
Dividends			300	
	55,121	1,345	300	£56,766
Less: Personal allowance	(4,895)			
	50,226	1,345	300	£51,871

Tax on non savings income

	£
£2,090 × 10%	209
£30,310 × 22%	6,668
£3,077 (£200 × 100/78 × 12) × 22%	677
£14,749 × 40%	5,900

Tax on Savings (excl. dividend) income

£1,345 × 40%	538

Tax on dividend income

£300 × 32.5%	98

	14,090
Less: Tax suffered	
Tax credit on dividend	(30)
Tax on interest	(269)
PAYE	(11,180)
Income tax payable	2,611

Workings

1   **Taxable percentage for car and fuel benefits**

CO_2 emissions (rounded down to nearest 5 below) 170g/km − 140 = 30
Divide by 5 = 6
Taxable % = 15% + 6% = 21%

2   **Taxable cheap loan**

Average method

$$\frac{£20,000 + £14,000}{2} = £17,000 \times (5\% - 1.5\%) = £595$$

BPP
PROFESSIONAL EDUCATION

Strict method would give same result:

	£
£20,000 × 6/12 × (5% − 1.5%) =	350
£14,000 × 6/12 × (5% − 1.5%) =	245
	595

(b)   'Tax Help For You'
16 The Road
London
England

John Hunt
22 The Street
Anywhere
England

28 September 2006

Dear John

Income tax return

Further to your letter of 16 September 2006, I am writing to let you know that I will need the following information and documents in order to complete your income tax return.

1   *Forms P60 and P11D*

Both of these forms should have been supplied to you by your employer. Form P60 will give me details of your salary and tax deducted from it. Form P11D will give me the details I need regarding your company car and private medical insurance.

2   *Bank and Building Society Certificates of annual interest earned*

These will provide the details I need regarding your taxable interest and the tax deducted from it.

3   *Annual pension statement*

This will give me the details I need of your pension payments and of any tax withheld at source from the payments.

4   *Receipted subscription notice*

This will show me details of the subscription you have paid.

I do not need any details of either your mortgage payments or of the interest arising on your ISA account. This is because there is no tax relief for mortgage payments and the interest arising on your ISA account is tax free.

Your completed tax return must be submitted to HMRC by 31 January 2007. Had you wanted HMRC to calculate your tax for you, you would need to submit your return by 30 September 2006.

Any outstanding tax is due for payment on 31 January 2007. Tax is only normally collected via a PAYE code if the outstanding amount is less than £2,000 and the return has been submitted by 30 September following the tax year concerned.

A fixed penalty of £100 applies if your tax return is not submitted by 31 January 2007. This penalty rises to £200 if the return is more than six months late. Interest is charged on a daily basis in respect of any tax paid late and there is an additional 5% surcharge if tax is paid more than 28 days late.

Finally, in response to the final point in your letter, a husband and wife are taxed independently so there will be no need for us to consider your wife's income when completing your tax return.

I look forward to meeting you but in the meantime, if you have any further queries please do not hesitate to contact me.

Yours sincerely

Peter Jones

Marking guide

		Marks	
(a)	Salary	½	
	Bonus	1	
	Car benefit	2½	
	Fuel benefit	1	
	Medical cover	1	
	Taxable cheap loan	2	
	Bank interest	1	
	Building society interest	1	
	Dividends	1	
	Personal allowance	½	
	Extended basic rate band	1½	
	Tax at 10%, 22%, 40%, 32½%	2	
	Tax credit on dividend	½	
	Tax on interest	1	
	PAYE	½	
			17
(b)	Forms P11D and P60	2	
	Bank and building society certificates	1	
	Annual pension statement	1	
	Receipted subscription notice	1	
	Mortgage/ISA	1	
	Return filing date	2	
	Tax due date	2	
	Penalties	2	
	Wife's income	1	
	Presentation	2	
			15
			32

6   JOSH GIBBONS

(a) Josh Gibbons is a qualified carpenter. He is about to undertake some work for a major UK company.

He has always been classed as self-employed but the company wants to treat him as an employee.

You are required to explain the factors that could be taken into account when deciding whether he is employed or self-employed.   (12 marks)

(b) If it is agreed that Josh is to be treated as an employee he will contribute to the company pension scheme.

You are required to give outline details of the taxation implications of occupational pension schemes for both Josh and the company.   (8 marks)

(20 marks)

6   ANSWER: JOSH GIBBONS

(a)   The factors to consider in deciding whether someone is employee or self-employed for income tax purposes are as follows.

  (i)   **How much control is exercised over the way work is done?** The greater the control, the more likely it is that the worker is an employee.

  (ii)   **Does the worker provide his own equipment?** That would indicate self-employment.

  (iii) **If the worker hires his own helpers,** that indicates self-employment.

  (iv)   If the **worker can profit by his own sound management,** or lose money through errors, that indicates self-employment.

  (v)   If there is a **continuing obligation to provide work for the worker,** and an obligation on the worker to do whatever job is offered next, that indicates employment.

  (vi)   If the **worker accepts work from many independent sources,** that indicates self-employment.

  (vii) If the **worker can work whenever he chooses,** that indicates self-employment.

These tests are summed up in the general rule that there is **employment when there is a contract of service, and self-employment when there is a contract for services.**

(b)   Occupational pension schemes can be of two kinds: Revenue approved and unapproved. Approved schemes have significant tax advantages that have made them very popular.

If a scheme is Revenue approved:

  •   **Contributions made by the employee are deductible from his earnings** (up to a limit of 15% of gross earnings, with gross earnings limited to the earnings cap).

  •   The **employer's contributions actually paid** (not merely provided for) are **deductible in calculating profits subject to tax** (although deductions for large contributions above the normal level may be spread over several years).

  •   The **employer's contributions are not regarded as taxable benefits** for the employee and are **not earnings for NICs purposes.**

  •   The fund of contributions, and the income and gains arising from their investment, are not, in general, liable to tax. It is this long-term tax-free accumulation of funds that makes approved schemes so beneficial.

  •   **Provision can be made for a lump sum to be paid on the employee's death in service.** Provided that it does not exceed four times his final remuneration, it is tax-free.

  •   A **tax-free lump sum may be paid to the employee on retirement.**

The following limits apply to an approved occupational pension scheme.

  •   The **maximum** pension is normally **two thirds of the individual's final remuneration,** being calculated as one sixtieth for each year of service, with a maximum of 40 years.

  •   A scheme may provide for part of the pension to be taken **as a lump sum.** The **maximum lump sum is 1.5 times final remuneration,** being calculated as 3/80 for each year of service, with a maximum of 40 years.

The Revenue have discretion to approve schemes which do not comply with these limits. In particular, many schemes provide for a pension of two thirds of final salary after less than 40 years service.

The earnings cap

An earnings cap applies to tax-approved occupational pension schemes. The cap is £105,600 for 2005/06.

The earnings cap has two consequences.

- The maximum pension payable from an approved scheme is the cap × 2/3.
- The maximum tax-free lump sum is the cap × 1.5.

Marking guide

		Marks
(a)	For/of services	3
	For each criteria 1.5 marks - maximum of 6 × 1.5 =	9
		12
(b)	Tax deductible (15%)	1
	Tax	1
	Employers contributions	1
	Benefit	1
	Lump sums	1
	Earnings cap	1
	Pension limit	1
	Lump sum limit	1
		8
		20

---

7   QUESTION WITH HELP: ADJUSTMENT OF PROFIT

George carries on a trade as a drapery wholesaler making up accounts to 31 January in each year.

His trading and profit and loss account for the year ended 31 January 2006 is as follows.

		£	£
Sales			825,630
Less:	opening stock	105,966	
	purchases	720,273	
		826,239	
	less closing stock	83,203	
			743,036
Gross profit			82,594
Less:	wages	22,504	
	rent, rates, light and heat	26,492	
	repairs	7,206	
	professional charges	1,000	
	sundry expenses	3,962	
	travelling and entertaining	9,041	
	Impairment losses	1,336	
	depreciation	2,874	
			74,415
Profit for the year			8,179

Notes

			£
(a)	Professional charges		
	Debt collection		150
	Accountancy		760
	Advice regarding trading agreement		90
			1,000
(b)	Sundry expenses		
	Chamber of Commerce subscription		22
	Donations to local charities		18
	Sundry allowable expenses		3,922
			3,962
(c)	Travelling and entertaining		
	General travelling including travellers' car expenses		7,527
	Expenses of George's car		640
	Entertaining		874
			9,041
(d)	Impairment losses		
	Amounts written off trade debtors		541
	Amounts written off – non-trade debtors		795
			1,336

It has been agreed that the private use by George of his car is 25%.

Required

Compute the adjusted profit for income tax purposes based on these accounts. Ignore capital allowances

> *If you are stuck, look at the next page for detailed help as to how you should tackle this question.*

APPROACHING THE ANSWER

Use this answer plan to construct your answer if you are stuck.

Step 1   You are asked to compute the adjusted profit. You should therefore start by setting out a pro forma, starting with the accounts profit and leaving plenty of space for adding disallowable items, and rather less space for deducting any items not taxable under Schedule D Case I. It does not matter if you end up not using all the space.

Step 2   You should then work systematically through the detailed profit and loss account and the notes, taking any items for which an adjustment is needed to your pro forma as you go.

Step 3   To deal with the car expenses you must bring together two pieces of information (the amount and the private use percentage) which are separated in the question.

Step 4   Finally, add up your adjusted profit computation.

7   **ANSWER TO QUESTION WITH HELP: ADJUSTMENT OF PROFIT**

ADJUSTED PROFIT COMPUTATION

	£	£
Net profit per accounts		8,179
Add: car expenses (25% × £640)	160	
entertaining	874	
Non-trade debtors W/O	795	
depreciation	2,874	
		4,703
Adjusted trading profit		12,882

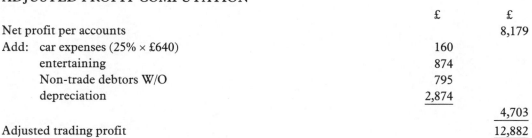

8   JACKIE SMITH

(a) Jackie Smith started her picture framing business on 1 May 2001. Due to falling profits she ceased to trade on 28 February 2006.

Her profits for the whole period of trading were as follows.

	£
1 May 2001 – 31 July 2002	18,000
1 August 2002 – 31 July 2003	11,700
1 August 2003 – 31 July 2004	8,640
1 August 2004 – 31 July 2005	6,800
1 August 2005 – 28 February 2006	4,100

Jackie has no other income in any of the periods concerned.

Required

Calculate the total assessable profits for each of the tax years concerned.

You are to assume that ALL possible claims are made.   (8 marks)

(b) List seven factors, which may be taken into account, when deciding whether an individual is to be treated as self-employed or as an employee.   (7 marks)

(15 marks)

Helping hand

Overlap profits can be relieved in the final year of trade.

In part (b) you are asked to list **seven** factors. To maximise your marks ensure you list seven different factors and that you help your marker by numbering these factors (1) to (7).

---

8   ANSWER: JACKIE SMITH

(a)

	£	£
2001/02		
1st year – 1.5.01 to 5.4.02		
11/15 × £18,000		13,200
2002/03		
2nd year 12 months to 31.7.02 (1.8.01 - 31.7.02)		
12/15 × £18,000		14,400
Overlap period is 1.8.01 to 5.4.02		
ie 8/15 × £18,000 = £9,600		
2003/04		
3rd year y/e 31.7.03		11,700
2004/05		
y/e 31.7.04		8,640
2005/06		
y/e 31.7.05	6,800	
p/e 28.2.06	4,100	
	10,900	
Less: overlap relief	(9,600)	1,300

(b)   Seven factors to consider in deciding whether someone is employed or self-employed for income tax purposes are as follows:

(i)   **How much control is exercised** over the way work is done? The greater the control, the more likely it is that the worker is an employee.

(ii)   **Does the worker provide his own equipment**? That would indicate self-employment.

(iii) **If the worker hires his own helpers,** that indicates self employment.

(iv)   If the **worker can profit by his own sound management,** or lose money through errors, that indicates self employment.

(v)   If there is a **continuing obligation to provide work** for the worker, and an obligation on the employer to do whatever job is offered next, that indicates employment.

(vi)   If the **worker accepts work from many independent sources,** that indicates self employment.

(vii) If the **worker can work whenever he chooses,** that indicates self-employment.

Marking guide

			Marks
(a)	2001/02		1
	2002/03		1
	Overlap profits		1
	2003/04		1
	2004/05		1
	2005/06		3
			8
(b)	1 mark for any relevant factor – max 7		7
			15

What the examiner said

'This was again a two-part question but this time involving sole traders. Markers reported that candidates either did very well on part (a), or very well on part (b), few doing well on both parts.

Part (a) required candidates to calculate the profits to be assessed in the relevant tax years of a business life cycle. The figures given were for opening and closing years, which involved the use of overlap profits in the early years being utilised on cessation. The biggest mistake here was that despite the question asking for TAX YEARS many candidates just copied the figures onto their answer booklet and made no attempt to allocate them to correct tax years. This approach earned few marks. Candidates must in future learn that they MUST quote tax years when dealing with individuals, merely quoting accounting periods will not score many, if any, marks.

Part (b) required a theory answer giving factors that would help to determine if an individual was to be treated as an employee or as self employed. Once again markers were 'generous' where candidates lacked clarity in their answers. Candidates failed to score marks when they gave the 'consequences' of being an employee, eg NIC and PAYE being deducted. The point of the question was to help decide if these items should be deducted or not! As stated earlier this part of the question was either well answered or was a complete impossibility for some.'

9   **AMANDA COOKE (06/04)**

Amanda Cooke started in business as a self-employed clothes designer on 1 December 2002. She made up her first set of accounts to 31 May 2003 and annually thereafter. Her first two sets of adjusted trading profits after capital allowances were:

Period ended 31 May 2003	£4,260
Year ended 31 May 2004	£8,190

During her accounting year ended 31 May 2005 Amanda had the following results:

	£	£
Turnover		18,000
Cost of goods sold		(7,300)
Gross profit		10,700
Discounts received		300
Bank interest received		450
		11,450
Electricity	810	
Accountant's fees	280	
Depreciation	120	
Drawings	640	
Car expenses	1,840	(3,690)
Net profit		£7,760

Amanda works from home and 40% of the electricity costs relate to personal use.

Her car was purchased new in 2000 for £12,000 and had a value of £6,400 when it was introduced into the business on 1 December 2002. She uses the car 60% for business purposes.

Amanda's only other asset is a sewing machine, which had a written down tax value for capital allowance purposes of £240 on 1 June 2004.

Required

(a)   Calculate the maximum capital allowances that Amanda may claim for the year ended 31 May 2005.
                                                                        (3 marks)

(b)   Calculate the adjusted trading profits after capital allowances for the year ended 31 May 2005.
                                                                        (4 marks)

(c)   Calculate the assessable trading profits for the four years 2002/03 to 2005/06 inclusive.
                                                                        (5 marks)

(d)   Calculate the overlap profits for the openings years of assessment.
                                                                        (2 marks)

                                                                        (14 marks)

9   **ANSWER: AMANDA COOKE**

> **Tutorial note**. When you are asked for assessments in opening years, you should take care to show which years your assessments relate to.

(a)   **Capital allowances**

	Pool £	Private use car £		Allowances £
1.12.02 - 31.5.03				
Addition		6,400		
Less: WDA 6/12 × 25%		(800)	×60%	480
		5,600		
Y/e 31.5.04				
WDA @ 25%		(1,400)	×60%	880
Y/e 31.5.05				
TDWV b/f	240	4,200		
Less: WDA 25%	(60)	(1,050)	×60%	690
TWDV c/f	180	3,150		

Note: Strictly, the actual allowances for the first two periods of account do not need to be shown.

(b)   **Trading profits y/e 31.5.05**

	£	£
Net profit		7,760
Les: building society interest		(450)
		7,310
Add: private use electricity		
£810 × 40%	324	
Depreciation	120	
Drawings	640	
Private use car expenses		
£1,840 × 40%	736	1,820
		9,130
Less: capital allowances		(690)
Trading Income		8,440

(c)   Trading profits 2002/03 to 2005/06

2002/03

1st year - actual

	£	£
1.12.02 – 5.4.03		
4/6 × £4,260		2,840

2003/04

2nd year – 1st 12 months

	£	£
1.12.02 – 31.5.03	4,260	
1.6.03 – 30.11.03		
6/12 × £8,190	4,095	8,355

2004/05

3rd year – period of account ending in tax year

	£
Y/e 31.5.04	8,190

2005/06

	£
Y/e 31.5.05	8,440

BPP
PROFESSIONAL EDUCATION

(d) **Overlap profits**

		£
1.12.02 – 5.4.03		2,840
1.6.03 – 30.11.03		4,095
Total overlap profits		6,935

Marking guide

				Marks
(a)	Car	-	p/e 31.5.03	1
		-	y/e 31.5.04	½
		-	y/e 31.5.05	1
		-	y/e 31.5.05	½
	Plant	-	y/e 31.5.05	
				3
(b)	Adjustments - bank interest			½
	- electricity			1
	- depreciation			½
	- drawings			½
	- car			1
	- CAs			½
				4
(c)	2002/2003			1½
	2003/2004			1½
	2004/2005			1
	2005/2006			1
				5
(d)	1.12.02 – 5.9.03			1
	1.6.03 – 30.11.03			1
				2
				14

What the examiner said. This was a four-part question based on sole traders. The question requirements guided candidates through the calculation of capital allowances to the adjustment of profits and the appropriate trading income assessments.

The capital allowances calculation was made slightly complicated by the need to retrace the calculation of the written down value since its introduction into the business on 1 December 2002. This part threw many candidates but some reasonable attempt was made by most.

The adjustment of profit required minor changes as a result of private use and non-tax allowance deductions. This was done well by most candidates.

The third requirement was opening year assessments for the given profit figures. Candidates should be aware that it is difficult to earn marks if exact tax years are not stated – it is not enough to use statements such as year 1, year 2 etc. The years should have started with 2002-03 and finished with 2004-05 as required by the question.

Finally the calculation of overlap profits was required. This was done reasonably well by those who understood part (c), obviously if a candidate could not do part (c) then part (d) was not a possibility.

10   **QUESTION WITH HELP: PLANT AND INDUSTRIAL BUILDINGS**

Saruman is the sole proprietor of a small engineering business. He prepares accounts annually to 31 March.

Required

Calculate capital allowances for the purpose of trading income for the year ending 31 March 2006 based on the following information.

(a)   General pool brought forward on 1 April 2005   £52,000
      Tax written down value of motor car for Saruman's use on 1 April 2005   £600

      Private use of this car has been agreed with the Revenue at 25%.

      The following events occurred during the year ended 31 March 2006.

Disposals:	20 April 2005	-	Plant £12,000 (original cost £10,000)
	21 May 2005	-	Motor car for Saruman's own use £920 (original cost £1,896)
	20 June 2005	-	Plant £800 (original cost £3,000)
Additions:	1 May 2005	-	New plant £4,000
	21 May 2005	-	New car for Saruman's use £19,000
	1 October 2005	-	Estate car for use of sales representative £4,800

(b)   A new small factory was bought from a builder for a total cost of £40,000, including land £10,000 and office accommodation £3,000. The factory was purchased and brought into use on 10 September 2005.

> *If you are stuck, look at the next page for detailed help as to how you should tackle this question.*

APPROACHING THE ANSWER

Use this answer plan to construct your answer if you are stuck.

Step 1 When tackling a capital allowances computation, the first step is to set out the headings of the columns clearly, leaving plenty of space for items that need individual treatment (such as assets with private use).

Step 2 Deal systematically with the additions and disposals, and calculate the total for each column before working out the capital allowances available.

Step 3 Remember to adjust the 25% rate of WDA where necessary.

Step 4 Remember to take FYA where relevant and add the balance to the pool.

Step 5 Remember that where disposal proceeds exceed original cost the deduction for capital allowances purposes is limited to the cost. This means that only £10,000 is deducted for the disposal on 20 April 2005.

Step 6 When dealing with industrial buildings allowances, two dates are critical: the date the building is brought into use and the final day of the period of account. No WDAs are due before a building is brought into use and it is the use the building is put to on the final day of the period of account that determines whether an allowance is due for the relevant tax year.

10   ANSWER TO QUESTION WITH HELP: PLANT AND INDUSTRIAL BUILDINGS

CAPITAL ALLOWANCES COMPUTATION FOR THE YEAR ENDED 31 MARCH 2006

	FYA £	General Pool £	Saruman's car (75%) £	Allowances/ (charges) £
b/f		52,000	600	
Disposals (20.4.05)		(10,000)		
(20.6.05)		(800)		
		41,200		
(21.5.05)			(920)	
Balancing charge			(320) @ 75%	(240)
Additions (no FYAs on cars)				
(21.5.05)			19,000	
(1.10.05)		4,800		
		46,000		
WDA @ 25%		(11,500)	(3,000) @ 75%	13,750
		34,500	16,000	
Addition (1.5.05)	4,000			
FYA at 40%	(1,600)	1,600		1,600
TWDV c/f		36,100	16,000	15,110

The maximum WDA on the car is £3,000. This is then adjusted for private use for the actual allowances given.

The industrial building

	£
Cost excluding land	30,000
WDA 4%	(1,200)
WDV c/f	28,800

Total capital allowances are £15,110 + £1,200 = £16,310.

BPP
PROFESSIONAL EDUCATION

11 MISS FARRINGTON

Miss Farrington started to trade as a baker on 1 January 2003 and made up her first accounts to 30 April 2004. Adjusted profits before capital allowances are as follows.

	£
Period to 30 April 2004	16,000
Year to 30 April 2005	13,400

Miss Farrington incurred the following expenditure on plant and machinery.

Date	Item	£
4.1.03	General plant	3,835
1.3.03	Secondhand oven acquired from Miss Farrington's father	1,200
25.3.03	Delivery van	1,800
15.4.03	Typewriter	425
15.5.03	Car for Miss Farrington	2,600
1.1.04	General plant	800
30.4.04	Computer	1,945

In addition Miss Farrington brought into the business on 1 January 2003 a desk and other office furniture. The agreed value was £940.

The agreed private use of the car is 35%. Miss Farrington's business is a small enterprise for capital allowance purposes.

Required

Calculate the taxable profits for the first four tax years and the overlap profits carried forward.

(15 marks)

Helping hand

In a question like this, work out the capital allowances and then the trading profits for each period of account before you think about allocating profits to tax years.

Writing down allowances are time apportioned in a long period of account but first year allowances are not. The fact that the business is a small enterprise for capital allowance purposes means that first year allowances of 50% are available for the expenditure on the general plant bought on 1 January 2005.

---

11 ANSWER: MISS FARRINGTON

> **Helping hand**. Most of the expenditure in the first period of account qualified for a 40% FYA which is not pro-rated. Expenditure on the car qualifies for a writing down allowance which must be multiplied by $^{16}/_{12}$ to take account of the long period.

We must first work out the capital allowances.

	FYA £	Pool £	Car (65%) £	Allowances £
1.1.03 - 30.4.04				
Car			2,600	
WDA @ 25% × 16/12			(867)	564
Desk and office furniture	940			
General plant	3,835			
Secondhand oven	1,200			
Delivery van	1,800			
Typewriter	425			
	8,200			
FYA @ 40% (all pre 6.4.04)	(3,280)			3,280
		4,920	1,733	3,844
1.5.04 – 30.4.05				
WDA @ 25%		(1,230)	(433)	1,511
		3,690	1,300	
General plant (pre 6.4.05)	800			
FYA @ 50%	(400)			400
		400		
Computer (post 5.4.05)	1,945			
FYA @ 40%	(778)	1,167		778
		5,257	1,300	2,689

Profits are as follows.

Period	Profit £	Capital allowances £	Adjusted profit £
1.1.03 - 30.4.04	16,000	3,844	12,156
1.5.04 - 30.4.05	13,400	2,689	10,711

The taxable profits are as follows.

Year	Basis period	Working	Taxable profit £
2002/03	1.1.03 - 5.4.03	£12,156 × 3/16	2,279
2003/04	6.4.03 - 5.4.04	£12,156 × 12/16	9,117
2004/05	1.5.03 - 30.4.04	£12,156 × 12/16	9,117
2005/06	1.5.04 - 30.4.05		10,711

The overlap profits are the profits from 1 May 2003 to 5 April 2004: £12,156 × 11/16 =

12   JIM SMALL

Little Jim's bicycle sales and repair shop is owned by Jim Small and opened for business on 1 February 2003. The first set of accounts was made up to 31 May 2004. An adjusted profit, after capital allowances, of £8,000 was accepted by HMRC.

The second period of accounts was for the 12 months ended 31 May 2005 and showed a trading profit (before tax adjustments and capital allowances) of £2,400.

The accounts ended 31 May 2005 included the following items.

Expenditure

Depreciation £800.

Legal fees of £1,100. Of this £400 was for debt collecting, £300 for successful defence of an action against product quality and £400 for mortgage arrangements on his private residence.

£2,500 for building of a new storage house for his stock of bicycles. He started to use this storage house in July 2005.

Receipts

Discount received of £400.

An amount of £3,000 from an insurance company for the loss of stock in a fire.

£800 (net) for interest on his business bank account.

During the period 1 June 2004 to 31 May 2005 Jim took stock, valued at £285 from the shop for his own personal use. He has not paid for this. Jim's normal profit margin is 25%.

Jim owned a van before the business started that had cost him £6,000 in 2000 but was only worth £3,000 when he brought it into his business in February 2003. He uses the van 40% for private motoring.

On 18 April 2003 Jim spent £2,500 on new shop fittings and in June 2004 he purchased specialised equipment, for £1,120, to use in his repair service.

The next 12-month account period ending on 31 May 2006 is expected to show a trading loss of £6,000.

Required

(a)   Calculate the adjusted profit for the period ending 31 May 2005.   (9 marks)

(b)   Calculate the first four years of trading income (apportionment to be done in months).
                                                                                                    (5 marks)

(c)   Advise Jim Small as to how he can utilise the £6,000 loss expected in the period ending 31 May 2006 (you are NOT required to show any calculations).   (6 marks)

                                                                                                (20 marks)

Helping hand

Write down the basis periods for each tax year before trying to match them to profits.

---

12   ANSWER: JIM SMALL

> **Helping hand**
>
> Remember that the first tax year's assessable profits are on an actual basis and that generally no more than 12 months profits are assessable per tax year.

(a)   JIM SMALL
CALCULATION OF ADJUSTED PROFIT

	£	£
Profit per accounts		2,400
Add: depreciation	800	
legal fees re mortgage	400	
storage house	2,500	
goods for own use (285 × 100/75)	380	
		4,080
		6,480
Less: interest received	800	
capital allowances (W)	1,205	
		(2,005)
Adjusted profit		4,475

Working

Capital allowances

	FYA £	General machinery £	Private use Vans (60%) £	Total CAs £
1.2.2003 – 31.5.2004				
Additions				
Van (pre 6.4.04)	3,000			
FYA @ 40%	(1,200) × 60%			720
			1,800	
Shop fittings (pre 6.4.04)	2,500			
FYA @ 40%	(1,000)	1,500		1,000
				1,720
TWDV @ 31.5.04		1,500	1,800	
Y/e 31.5.2005				
WDA @ 25%		(375)	(450) × 60%	645
		1,125	1,350	
Addition	1,120			
FYA @ 50% (after 5.4.04)	(560)	560		560
TWDV c/f		1,685	1,350	
Total allowances				1,205

Note: **First year allowances are not pro-rated in the first long period of account. Writing down allowances would be pro-rated in a long period.**

(b) Trading income for first four years of trading.

16 months to 31.5.2004	£8,000
Y/e 31.5.2005	£4,475
1ˢᵗ tax year - 2002/03 – Actual	
1.2.03 - 5.4.03 2/16 × £8,000	£1,000
2ⁿᵈ tax year – 2003/04 –Actual	
6.4.03 – 5.4.04 12/16 × £8,000	£6,000
3ʳᵈ tax year – 2004/05	
12 months to 31.5.04 12/16 × £8,000	£6,000
4ᵗʰ year –2005/06 CYB	
Y/e 31.5.05	£4,475

(c) *Use of loss relief*

There are two options for using loss relief.

(i) Under Section 380 of ICTA 1988 **the loss may be offset against the income of the tax year in which the loss was suffered (2006/07) and/or the previous tax year (2005/06).**

A claim for a loss must be made by the 31 January which is nearly 22 months after the end of the tax year of the loss, ie by 31 January 2009.

Jim cannot choose the amount of loss to relieve, thus it may have to be set against income which would otherwise have been covered by the personal allowance. However, he can choose whether to claim full relief in the current year and then relief in the preceding year for any remaining loss, or the other way round.

(ii) **Relief is available by carry forward** under section 385 for any loss not relieved under section 380. **Section 385 requires such losses to be set against the first available profits of the same trade.** Losses may be carried forward for any number of years.

Marking guide

			Marks
(a)	Add backs (except goods for own use)	$3 \times \frac{1}{2}$	
	Goods for own use	3	
	Bank interest deduction	$\frac{1}{2}$	
	Capital allowances	$\underline{4}$	
			9
(b)	First three years	$3 \times 1\frac{1}{2}$	
	Fourth year	$\underline{\frac{1}{2}}$	
			5
(c)	Section 380	4	
	Section 385	$\underline{2}$	
			6
			$\underline{\underline{20}}$

What the examiner said

'The answers to this question were split fairly evenly between being either very good or very poor. This was a common question testing adjustments of trading and the assessment of opening years for a sole trade. Those candidates who scored poorly seemed to have no idea of the current year basis of trading income – an area which will be tested regularly in the future.'

13   QUESTION WITH HELP: USE OF LOSSES

The following information relates to Mr N who has run a shop since 1 July 2000.

Mr N's trading profits have been, or are expected to be, as follows:

		£
Year ended 30 June 2004	Profit	4,000
Year ended 30 June 2005	Loss	11,000
Year ended 30 June 2006	Profit (projected)	14,000

Mr N's other taxable income is as follows.

	£
2004/05	
Property business income	1,000 (loss)
2005/06	
Property business income	20,000
2006/07	
Property business income	12,000

Required

Calculate Mr N's income tax liability for 2004/05 to 2006/07 assuming that loss relief is claimed in the most efficient way.

Assume that the personal allowance and rates of tax applicable to 2005/06 apply to all the years involved.

> *If you are stuck, look at the next page for detailed help as to how you should tackle this question.*

APPROACHING THE ANSWER

Use this answer plan to construct your answer if you are stuck.

Step 1   You must first work out the year in which the loss arose and Mr N's options for relieving this loss. These should be listed, briefly stating the income against which the loss would be relieved.

Step 2   You must then choose the best form of loss relief. You should find that there is only one option which both gives relief quickly and does not set the loss against income which would otherwise be covered by the personal allowance.

Step 3   Having made your choice, you should set out a working with a column for each year covered and a line for each source of income, a line for loss relief and a line for the personal allowance. Also allow space for sub-totals.

Step 4   You can now insert the figures from the question into your working, and get the taxable income for each year.

Step 5   Finally, work out the income tax.

Step 6   If you set out the alternative loss relief claims clearly, the computation should have been straightforward. It is important to practise giving finished answers to questions which require you to list alternative claims; do not assume that a scrappy note will do and that neatness and clarity will come naturally in the real examination.

13   ANSWER TO QUESTION WITH HELP: USE OF LOSSES

The loss of £11,000 is a loss for 2005/06.

Possible loss relief claims are:

(a)   Against total income for 2004/05
(b)   Against total income for 2005/06
(c)   Under (a) and then the remaining loss under (b)
(d)   Against the trading income of £14,000 in 2006/07

(a) (and therefore (c)) should be avoided, as loss relief in 2004/05 would cover income which would in any case be covered by the personal allowance. Both (b) and (d) save tax at 22%. However, as (b) saves tax more quickly it is more beneficial from a cashflow point of view.

The property business income loss arising in 2004/05 is carried forward to set against future property business profits.

	2004/05 £	2005/06 £	2006/07 £
Trading income	4,000	0	14,000
Property business income (£20,000 – £1,000)	0	19,000	12,000
	4,000	19,000	26,000
Less s 380 loss relief	0	(11,000)	0
	4,000	8,000	26,000
Less personal allowance	(4,895)	(4,895)	(4,895)
Taxable income	0	3,105	21,105
Income tax on non-savings income			
£2,090/£2,090 × 10%	0	209	209
£1,015/£19,015 × 22%	0	223	4,183
	0	432	4,392

14   QUESTION WITH HELP: PARTNERSHIPS

Clare and Justin commenced trading in partnership on 1 October 2002, initially sharing profits and losses as to Clare one third and Justin two thirds. They prepared their first set of accounts to 31 January 2003. Accounts were prepared to 31 January thereafter.

Malcolm joined the partnership on 1 May 2004. From this date the profit and losses were shared equally. On 31 December 2005, Justin resigned with Clare and Malcolm continuing to share profits equally. Trading profits were as follows:

	£
1.10.02 - 31.01.03	26,400
y/e 31.01.04	60,000
y/e 31.01.05	117,000
y/e 31.01.06	108,108

Required

Calculate the amount on which each partner will be taxed in respect of the partnership profits for 2002/03 to 2005/06 inclusive. Show any overlap profits that remain unrelieved.

> *If you are stuck, look at the next page for detailed help as to how you should tackle this question.*

APPROACHING THE ANSWER

Use this answer plan to construct your answer if you are stuck.

Step 1 You should start by dividing the profits for each period of account between the partners in accordance with the profit sharing ratio for that period.

Step 2 Next you can work out how much profit should be taxed in each tax year. Apply the opening and closing year rules to each partner individually according to when he or she joins or leaves the partnership.

Step 3 Each partner has their own overlap profits. These can be relieved when the partner concerned leaves the partnership.

14   ANSWER TO QUESTION WITH HELP: PARTNERSHIPS

Each partners share of the profits is

	Total £	Clare £	Justin £	Malcolm £
1.10.02-31.1.03	26,400	8,800	17,600	0
Y/e 31.1.04	60,000	20,000	40,000	0

Y/e 31.1.05

1.2.04-30.4.04				
(3/12 × £117,000)	29,250		9,750	19,500	0
1.5.04-31.1.05				
(9/12 × £117,000)	87,750		29,250	29,250	29,250
		117,000	39,000	48,750	29,250

Y/e 31.1.06

1.2.05-31.12.05				
(11/12 × £108,108)	99,099		33,033	33,033	33,033
1.1.06-31.1.06				
(1/12 × £108,108)	9,009		4,505	0	4,504
		108,108	37,538	33,033	37,537

The partners will be taxed on the above profits in the following tax years.

	Clare £	Justin £	Malcolm
2002/03 (1.10.02-5.4.03)			
1.10.02-31.1.03	8,800	17,600	
1.2.03-5.4.03 (2/12 × (£20,000/£40,000)	3,333	6,667	
	12,133	24,267	
2003/04 (Y/e 31.1.04)	£20,000	£40,000	
2004/05			
(Y/e 31.1.05)	£39,000	£48,750	
(1.5.04-5.4.05)			£
1.5.04-31.1.05			29,250
1.2.05-5.4.05 (2/12 × £37,537)			6,256
			35,506
2005/06			
(y/e 31.1.06)	£37,538		£37,537
(1.2.05-31.12.05)		33,033	
less: overlap relief		(6,667)	
		26,366	

Justin's overlap profits were relieved in the year he left the partnership. Clare and Malcolm have overlap profits that remain unrelieved of £3,333 and £6,256 respectively.

15   BOB, ANNIE AND JOHN

Bob, Annie and John started their partnership on 1 June 2000 and make accounts up to 31 May each year. The accounts have always shown taxable profits.

For the period up to 31 January 2005 each partner received a salary of £15,000 per annum and the remaining profits were shared 50% to Bob and 25% each to Annie and John. There was no interest on capital or drawings.

Bob left the partnership on 1 February 2005. The profit sharing ratio, after the same salaries, changed to 50% each to Annie and John.

On 1 August 2005 Susan was admitted as a partner with an annual salary of £12,000. Annie and John are to keep the same salary of £15,000 each and remaining profits are to be divided 40% each to Annie and John and 20% to Susan.

Profits for the years ending 31 May 2005 and 31 May 2006 were £90,000 and £120,000 respectively.

Required

Calculate each partner's share of the profits for the periods to 31 May 2005 and 31 May 2006 respectively. (Allocation should be done on a monthly basis.)   **(18 marks)**

Helping hand

Allocate salaries first, then the balance of profits in the stated ratios. Don't forget to pro-rate salaries when you are looking at periods of less than 12 months.

---

15 **ANSWER: BOB, ANNIE AND JOHN**

(a) *P/e 31.5.05*

	Bob £	Annie £	John £	Total £
1.6.04 – 31.1.05				
Salaries £15,000 × 8/12	10,000	10,000	10,000	30,000
Balance				
£(90,000 × 8/12 – 30,000) = £30,000	15,000	7,500	7,500	30,000
1.2.05 – 31.5.05				
Salaries £15,000 × 4/12	n/a	5,000	5,000	10,000
Balance				
£(90,000 × 4/12 – 10,000) = £20,000	n/a	10,000	10,000	20,000
Totals	25,000	32,500	32,500	90,000

(b) *P/e 31.5.06*

	Annie £	John £	Susan £	Total £
1.6.05 – 31.7.05				
Salaries £15,000 × 2/12	2,500	2,500	n/a	5,000
Balance				
£(120,000 × 2/12 – 5,000) = £15,000	7,500	7,500	n/a	15,000
1.8.05 – 31.5.06				
Salaries £15,000 × 10/12	12,500	12,500		25,000
£12,000 × 10/12			10,000	10,000
Balance				
£(120,000 × 10/12 – 35,000) = £65,000	26,000	26,000	13,000	65,000
Totals	48,500	48,500	23,000	120,000

Marking guide

	Marks
1.6.04 – 31.1.05	
Salaries	2
Balance	2
1.2.05 – 31.5.05	
Salaries	2
Balance	2
Totals	1
1.6.05 – 31.7.05	
Salaries	2
Balance	2
1.8.05 – 31.5.06	
Salaries	2
Balance	2
Totals	1
	18

What the examiner said

'Many papers include a question which can be regarded as a gift – this was such a question for many candidates. Indeed in some cases it was instrumental in being the main factor for passing the paper. There were many 100% correct answers but it was that type of question where you either scored relatively well or very poorly. For the most the former applied.

In this question the main problem was to split each period into two, taking account of the changed circumstances, allocating pro-rated wages for each sub period and then apportioning the balance of the profits for each sub period across the partners involved.'

16   CHARLES, MEG AND RODNEY (12/04)

(a)   Charles, Meg and Rodney have been in partnership for several years making up their accounts to 31 December annually. Profits have always been shared equally after allocation of salaries of £10,000 and £8,000 to Charles and Meg respectively and interest on capital of 5% to each of the three partners.

The partners have capital invested amounting to:

Charles	£20,000
Meg	£16,000
Rodney	£12,000

On 30 June 2005 Rodney left the partnership and withdraw his capital to start his own business. The remaining two partners continued with the same salaries and interest on capital, sharing any balance equally between them.

Rodney had overlap profits of £6,000 available from the opening years of the partnership.

The adjusted profit of the partnership for tax purposes for the accounting year ending 31 December 2005 was £120,000.

Required:

(i)   Calculate the profit share attributable to each partner for the accounting period ending 31 December 2005.   (8 marks)

(ii)   Calculate Rodney's trading income for his final year of assessment.

(2 marks)

(b)   Rodney started his new business on 1 August 2005 and made up his first set of accounts for the period ended 31 March 2006.

He purchased a new factory for use in the business on 1 September 2005, which was taken into industrial use immediately. The factory was purchased for £362,000.

	£
Land	90,000
Factory structure	180,000
Legal fees	10,000
Tunnelling	12,000
Administration office	70,000
Total	362,000

Required

(i)   Calculate the allowable cost for industrial buildings allowance (IBA) purposes.

(6 marks)

(ii)   Calculate the IBA available for the accounting period ending 31 March 2005.

(2 marks)

(18 marks)

16   ANSWER: CHARLES, MEG AND RODNEY

> **Tutorial Note.** Take care not to forget to pro-rate salaries and interest in a short period.
>
> Remember to time apportion the 4% Industrial Building Allowance according to the length of the accounts, not according to the number of months the factory has been in use.

(a) (i)   **Profit share**
         Year ended 31 December 2005

	Total £	Charles £	Meg £	Rodney £
1.1.05-30.6.05 (6/12)				
Salaries ($\times$ 6/12)	9,000	5,000	4,000	
Interest on capital ($\times$ 5% $\times$ 6/12)	1,200	500	400	300
Balance (1:1:1)	49,800	16,600	16,600	16,600
	60,000			
1.7.05-31.12.05 (6/12)				
Salaries ($\times$ 6/12)	9,000	5,000	4,000	
Interest on capital ($\times$ 5% $\times$ 6/12)	900	500	400	
Balance (1:1)	50,100	25,050	25,050	
	60,000			
Total for y/e 31.12.05		52,650	50,450	16,900

(ii)   **Rodney's trading income**

Fiscal year	Basis		Trading income £	£
2005/06	Closing year basis			
	Tax remainder (1.1.05 – 30.6.05)		16,900	
	Less: overlap profits		(6,000)	
				10,900

(b) (i)   **Rodney's factory – allowable costs**

	£
Factory cost	180,000
Legal fees (note)	10,000
Tunnelling	12,000
	202,000

Note. Unless specified assume legal fees relate to allowable costs.

Land never qualifies for Industrial Buildings Allowance (IBA).

Administration office is non-industrial expenditure. It can be included if it costs less than or equal to 25% of the total qualifying cost.

$$\frac{\text{Non-industrial}}{\text{Total cost}} = \frac{\text{Admin office}}{\text{Factory} + \text{legal fees} + \text{tunnel} + \text{admin office}}$$

$$= \frac{70,000}{180,000 + 10,000 + 12,000 + 70,000}$$

$$= 25.7\% > 25\%$$

Therefore, administration office is not eligible for IBAs as the cost of this non-industrial part is greater than 25% of the total qualifying cost.

(ii)   **Rodney's IBA for 8 month period ending 31 March 2006**

£202,000 $\times$ 4% $\times$ 8/12 = £5,387

PROFESSIONAL EDUCATION

Marking guide				Marks
(a)	(i)	Salaries	2	
		Interest on capital	2½	
		Profit share	2½	
		Total	1	
	(ii)	Fiscal year	½	
		Closing year rules	1½	
				10
(b)	(i)	Allowable costs	3	
		Land	1	
		Admin office	2	
	(ii)	4% pa IBA	1	
		Time-apportioned by 8/12	1	
				8
				18

What the examiner said

'Part (a) of this question required a simple partnership profit share allocation. This involves little tax knowledge and simply involved following the 'instructions' in the question. Many candidates scored full marks and many more only failed to score full marks because of silly calculation errors.

Part (b) was on the allowable cost of a building for industrial buildings allowance. A common mistake was to leave out the office without saying why. In this type of question candidates must show their workings if they are to get full marks. In general answers were of a mixed standard ranging from full knowledge to complete guesswork allowing land and legal fees and nothing else.

Finally the WDA is 4% per annum, where the accounting period is less than twelve months long then the WDA is restricted to that length ie. 8/12 in this question. Many of those that did restrict it, incorrectly limited it to 7/12 being the period of ownership rather than the length of the accounting period'.

17   MCBETH, MCDUFF AND MCBRIDE (PILOT PAPER)

(a) Gary McBeth was a partner in McBeth, McDuff and McBride, a firm of carpenters based in Scotland. The partnership had been in existence since October 2002.

On 31 October 2005 Gary decided to leave the partnership and start his own business.

The partnership has always made up accounts to 31 December annually and had agreed that profits should be shared 50% to McBeth and 25% to each of the other partners. Each partner was paid an annual salary of £9,600 and interest on capital of 2%. The partners had contributed capital of £24,000, £18,000 and £12,000 respectively to the business.

After Gary's departure the remaining two partners carried on the partnership with the same salaries and interest on capital and sharing the remaining profit equally.

Recent adjusted profits have been:

Year to 31 December 2004:   £48,000
Year to 31 December 2005:   £54,000

Gary had unused overlap profits of £6,000.

You are required to:

(i) Calculate each partner's share of the adjusted profit for the year ended 31 Decembers 2005; and   (8 marks)

(ii) Calculate Gary's final trading income assessment for tax year 2005/06.

(2 marks)

(b) Gary's new small business was started on 1 November 2005 and his first set of accounts was made up to 31 May 2006. He registered for VAT from the first day of business.

Gary purchased a secondhand combined workshop/storeroom for use in his carpentry business on 1 November 2005 for £120,000. This had cost the original owner £90,000 on 1 November 2001 and had always been used for a qualifying industrial purpose up to the date of sale. Both of these figures are exclusive of VAT.

On 24 November 2005 Gary purchased plant and machinery for £52,581 (inclusive of VAT) and a motorcar for £14,000 (inclusive of VAT) The car was used 60% for business and 40% for private purposes. It was not a low emission motorcar. On 1 February 2006 Gary purchased a computer for £7,520 (inclusive of VAT) which he uses 100% for business purposes.

Gary's adjusted profits before capital allowances for his first period were £44,500.

You are required to:

(i) Calculate the maximum capital allowances for both plant and machinery and industrial buildings available to Gary in his first period of account.   (11 marks)

(ii) Calculate Gary's trading income for the tax year 2005/06 on the assumption that he claims the maximum capital allowances available.   (3 marks)

(24 marks)

17   ANSWER: McBETH, McDUFF AND McBRIDE

> **Helping hand.** Take care not to forget to pro-rate salaries and interest in a short period.

(a)   (i)   *Year to 31 December 2005*

   1.1.05-31.10.05(10/12)

	Total £	*McBeth* £	*McDuff* £	*McBride* £
Salaries (10/12)	24,000	8,000	8,000	8,000
Interest (10/12)	900	400	300	200
Balance	20,100	10,050	5,025	5,025
Total (10/12)	45,000	18,450	13,325	13,225

   1.11.05-31.12.05 (2/12)

	Total £		*McDuff* £	*McBride* £
Salaries (2/12)	3,200		1,600	1,600
Interest (2/12)	100		60	40
Balance	5,700		2,850	2,850
Total (2/12)	9,000		4,510	4,490
Totals	54,000	18,450	17,835	17,715

   (ii)   Gary McBeth (2005/06)

	£
Basis period 1.1.05-31.10.05	18,450
Less: overlap relief	(6,000)
	12,450

(b)   (i)   **Industrial buildings allowance**

   IBAS available on lower of:

   (1)   Cost   £90,000
   (2)   Proceeds   £120,000

   ie £90,000

   Over remaining tax life, 21 years

   ie $\dfrac{90,000}{21}$ = £4,286 per annum.

   In the seven month period to 31.5.06 IBAs are (£4,286 × 7/12) £2,500

   Plant and machinery

	FYA £	*Pool* £	*Expensive car (60%)* £	*Allowance* £
Addition			14,000	
WDA (£3,000 × 7/12)			(1,750)(60%)	1,050
Addition (£52,581 × 40/47)	44,750			
FYA @ 40%	(17,900)			17,900
		26,850		
Addition (£7,520 × 40/47)	6,400			
FYA @ 40%	(2,560)	3,840		2,560
		30,690	12,250	21,510

   Total capital allowances
   £2,500 + £21,510 = £24,010

Tutorial notes

1. Since Gary is registered for VAT, he will be able to reclaim input tax on the business only use assets. Therefore, a VAT exclusive amount needs to be used for the CAs. This is calculated by taking 100/117.5 of the VAT inclusive price – equivalent to 40/47. However, the input tax on the car will not be recoverable so the VAT inclusive amount is used.

2. WDA are time apportioned in a short period of account. FYA are not.

(ii)   **7 months to 31 May 2006**   £

Profits   44,500
Less: Capital allowances   (24,010)
                                                                   20,490

2005/06 (1.11.05-5.4.06)

$5/7 \times £20,490 = £14,636$

Marking guide				Marks
(a)	(i)	*Jan-Oct*		
		Salaries		1
		Interest		1½
		Balance		1½
		Nov-Dec		
		Salary		1
		Interest		1
		Balance		1
		Totals		1
				8
	(ii)	Gary Mcbeth		2
(b)	(i)	*IBAs*		
		On cost		1
		Remaining life		1
		Seven month period		1
				3
		Expensive car addition		1
		WDA – car		2
		P/M / Computer additions		2
		FYAs		3
				8
	(ii)	Adjusted profit		1
		2005/06		2
				3
				24

18   LODGERS

You have received the following letter from a client.

> 12 Ash Street
> Anytown
> AN4 7LQ
>
> H Jones
> Technicians & Co
> 14 Duke Street
> Notown
> NT4 5AZ
>
> 3 October 2005
>
> Dear Hilary
>
> A friend of mine says she takes in lodgers, who stay for about a year, but she doesn't have to pay any tax on the rent she collects. I'd like to do the same. Can you tell me how this tax dodge works?
>
> Yours sincerely
>
> *David Green*
>
> David Green

Required

Write a reply to this letter.   **(15 marks)**

Helping hand

Marks will be awarded for letter format. Before you start, plan your answer. Think about who you are writing to. Your reply must be phrased in appropriate 'lay-man' terms so that the recipient will easily understand it.

BPP
PROFESSIONAL EDUCATION

18   **ANSWER: LODGERS**

Helping hand

The tone of the letter, and the use of the phrase 'tax dodge', should have made it clear to you that Mr Green is fairly ignorant of tax matters. A simple reply was therefore appropriate.

Technicians & Co
14 Duke Street
Notown
NT4 5AZ

D Green Esq
12 Ash Street
Anytown
AN4 7LJ

5 October 2005

Dear David

Thank you for your letter of 3 October.

Your friend is taking advantage of the **rent a room** scheme. This is a scheme to encourage people to let out spare rooms in their houses. It is part of UK tax law, so it is not in any sense a 'dodge'. It works as follows.

(a)   If an individual lets rooms, furnished, in his or her main residence, and **gross rents** (before deducting any expenses) **in a tax year do not exceed £4,250, the rents are not taxable** and any expenses are ignored.

(b)   The £4,250 limit is halved to £2,125 if anyone else (including the taxpayer's spouse) also receives income from letting accommodation in the property.

(c)   If **gross rents exceed** the limit (£4,250 or £2,125), the taxpayer can choose between the following alternatives.

   (i)   **Ignore the scheme and be taxed on rents minus expenses** in the ordinary way.
   (ii)   Be **taxed on gross rents minus £4,250** (or £2,125), and ignore expenses.

(d)   Even if gross rents do not exceed £4,250 (or £2,125), **the taxpayer may still choose to ignore the scheme**. This can be useful when expenses exceed rents. A loss can then be generated, and set against other rental income for tax purposes.

I hope that this letter clarifies the position for you.

Yours sincerely

Hilary Jones

Hilary Jones

19   PROPERTY BUSINESS INCOME

Peter starts to let out property on 1 July 2005. He has the following transactions.

(a)   On 1 July 2005, he lets a house which he has owned for several years. The tenant is required to pay an initial premium of £20,000 for a 30 year lease, and then to pay annual rent of £4,000, quarterly in advance. The house is let unfurnished.

(b)   On 1 October 2005 he buys a badly dilapidated house for £37,000. During October, he spends £8,000 on making the house habitable. He lets it furnished for £600 a month from 1 November 2005, but the tenant leaves on 31 January 2006. A new tenant moves in on 1 March 2006, paying £2,100 a quarter in arrears. Water rates are £390 a year, payable by Peter. Peter also pays buildings insurance of £440 for the period from 1 October 2005 to 31 August 2006. He financed the purchase (but not the repairs) with a bank loan at 10% interest. Peter decides to claim the renewals basis. He replaces some furniture on 1 May 2006, at a cost of £350. The tenant is responsible for all repair costs and council tax.

Required

Compute Peter's property business income for 2005/06.   **(11 marks)**

> **Helping hand**. Property business income is computed for tax years on an accruals basis. This means the income/expenses accruing in the tax year must be used in computing the income.

BPP
PROFESSIONAL EDUCATION

19   **ANSWER: PROPERTY BUSINESS INCOME**

PETER: PROPERTY BUSINESS INCOME

	£	£	£
First house			
Premium £20,000 × [1 − 0.02 (30 − 1)]			8,400
Rent £4,000 × 9/12			3,000
			11,400
Second house			
Rent £600 × 3		1,800	
Rent £2,100 × 1/3		700	
		2,500	
Less: water rates £390 × 6/12	195		
insurance £440 × 6/11	240		
interest £37,000 × 10% × 6/12	1,850		
repairs: capital	0		
furniture: in 2006/07	0		
		(2,285)	
Property business income			215
			11,615

20   JESSICA HUMPHRIES

(a) Jessica Humphries is a 46-year-old married woman working for a large UK resident company.

Jessica's annual salary had been £33,000 until 1 January 2006 on which date she received a 10% salary increase. Jessica received a bonus of £6,000 on 1 August 2005 this had been based on the company's profits for the period 1 January 2004 to 31 December 2004. She expects to receive a similar bonus but with a 10% increase in August 2006 which will be based on the company's results for the year end 31 December 2005.

Jessica's latest P60 shows PAYE deducted for the tax year 2005/2006 as £8,170.

During the tax year 2005/2006 Jessica received the following benefits from her employer:

- A relocation package totalling £9,000. This was in respect of a move from the company's Manchester office to its London headquarters.

- Accommodation for the period 1 November 2005 to 31 March 2006. The annual rateable value of the property was £4,200 and Jessica paid the company £200 rent per month. The property, which had been owned by the company since 1993, was valued at £120,000 when it was first made available to Jessica. Jessica had the use of furniture valued at £8,000 and the company paid all the utilities for the period, which amounted to £480.

- A £4,500 interest free loan for Jessica to purchase a season ticket for home to office travel. This was advanced on 1 November 2005 and the full amount is still outstanding.

- A £3,500 loan at 2% to help Jessica purchase a new car. This was advanced on 1 April 2005 and the full amount is still outstanding.

Jessica's car is a BMW, which she uses to drive to business meetings. During the tax year 2005/2006 she drove 10,000 miles of which 40% was on business related journeys. Jessica is paid 55p per mile for all of her business mileage. The company has no dispensation agreement with HMRC.

Jessica paid £3,510 (net) into a private pension plan during 2005/2006.

In addition to the above Jessica received the following investment income for 2005/2006:

- UK dividends of £450

- Building society interest of £2,000

- Dividend income from Individual Savings Account (ISA) investments made in the previous two years. This amounted to £270.

All three amounts were the cash amounts received.

Jessica's son, Gareth, is 16. He has a Saturday morning job and earned a total of £1,008 in 2005/2006. In addition he received dividends of £90 from UK share holdings and £80 (net) UK bank interest.

Required

For 2005/2006:

(i)   Calculate Jessica's income tax payable;   (20 marks)

(ii)   Calculate, and give an explanation for, the amount of tax reclaimable by Gareth.

                                                            (2 marks)

(b)   Jessica wishes to invest some money which she inherited, by buying accommodation in a popular UK holiday resort. She believes there are special conditions, which must be met for income derived from property to be treated as furnished holiday letting income.

Required

State the conditions necessary for a property to be assessed under the furnished holiday lettings rules.

(5 marks)

(c)   Jessica's friend Angela intends to let her spare room out to a lodger. She has agreed terms with a visiting builder to let the room to him for £100 a week starting on 1 April 2006. It is anticipated that the builder will stay for all of 2006/2007 and use 10% of the total household expenses, which are estimated to amount to £2,400 in total for 2006/2007.

Required

Calculate how much of the amounts paid to Angela will be assessed as property business income in the year of assessment 2006/2007.

Assume that any reliefs available remain at the same level as for 2005/2006, and will be claimed in full. Your answer must show any alternative calculations for the assessable amounts and the amount finally to be assessed.

(4 marks)

(31 marks)

20 ANSWER: JESSICA HUMPHRIES

(a) (i) **Jessica Humphries income tax payable 2005/06**

	Non-savings income £	Savings excl dividends) income £	Dividend income £	Total income £
Salary (W1)	33,825			
Bonus-receipts basis	6,000			
Relocation (W2)	1,000			
Accommodation (W3)	1,687			
Expenses of accommodation	480			
Use of furniture (W4)	667			
Loans (W5)	199			
Mileage (W6)	600			
Earnings	44,458			
BSI £2,000 × $^{100}/_{80}$		2,500		
Dividends £450 × $^{100}/_{90}$			500	
	44,458	2,500	500	47,458
Less: PA	(4,895)			(4,895)
	39,563	2,500	500	42,563

Note. ISA income is tax-exempt

Tax	£
£2,000 × 10%	209
£(32,400 – 2,090) = 30,310 × 22%	6,668
£4,500 (W7) × 22%	990
£(39,563 – 32,400 – 4,500) = 2,663 × 40%	1,065
£2,500 × 40%	1,000
£500 × 32.5%	162
Tax liability	10,094
Less: PAYE	(8,170)
tax on BSI	(500)
tax on dividends	(50)
Tax payable	1,374

Workings

1 Salary

	£
£33,000 × 9/12	24,750
£36,300 × 3/12	9,075
	33,825

2 Relocation

	£
Amount paid	9,000
Less: maximum exempt	(8,000)
Taxable benefit	1,000

3   Accommodation

	£	£
Annual value	4,200	
Less: rental £200 × 12	(2,400)	
	1,800	
× ⁵/₁₂		750
Additional benefit		
MV of property (acquired more than 6 years before provision)	120,000	
Less:	(75,000)	
	45,000	
× 5%	2,250	
× ⁵/₁₂		937
Total accommodation benefit		1,687

4   Furniture value £8,000 × 20% = £1,600

	£
× ⁵/₁₂	667

5   Total loans exceed £5,000 so both are taxable

	£
Season ticket loan	
£4,500 × 5% × ⁵/₁₂	94
Car loan	
£3,500 × (5 – 2)%	105
	199

6   Mileage payments

	£
Amount paid	
4,000 × 55p	2,200
Less: statutory amount	
4,000 × 40p	(1,600)
Taxable benefit	600

7   Pension contribution

Gross contribution £3,510 × 100/78 = £4,500

(ii)   **Gareth Humphries – Income tax repayable 2005/06**

	Non-savings income £	Savings (excl dividends) income £	Dividend income £	Total income £
Salary	1,008			
BI £80 × ¹⁰⁰/₈₀		100		
Dividends £90 × ¹⁰⁰/₉₀			100	
	1,008	100	100	1,208
Less: PA	(1,008)	(100)	(100)	(1,208)
Taxable income	nil	nil	nil	nil

No tax payable

Repayable:

BI £100 × 20%   £20

No repayment of tax credit on dividend.

(b) **Furnished holiday letting**

For a property to be assessed under the furnished holiday letting rules it must be:

(i)   **Furnished** accommodation **let on commercial basis with a view to realisation of profit**

(ii)   Situated in the **UK**

(iii) **Available** for commercial letting to the public for not less than **140 days in a tax year**

(iv)   **Actually let for 70 days** within the 140 day period

(v)   **For at least 7 months** (including the 70 days) **not normally in the same occupation for more than 31 days**

(c) **Lodger**

Normal property business income

	£
Rent received	
£100 × 52	5,200
Less: expenses	
£2,400 × 10%	(240)
Taxable	4,960

Rent-a-room basis

	£
Rents	5,200
Less: exemption	(4,250)
Taxable	950

Elect for alternative basis to apply by 31.1.09

ie. Taxable   £950

Marking guide

		Marks	
(a) (i)	Salary	1½	
	Bonus	1	
	Relocation	1	
	Accommodation	4	
	Expenses	½	
	Furniture	1	
	Loans	2	
	Mileage	1	
	BSI	1	
	Dividends	1	
	ISA – exempt	1	
	PA	½	
	Tax	3	
	PAYE/BSI/dividends	1½	20
(ii)	Nil tax to pay	½	
	BI repayable	½	
	Dividend credit not repayable	1	2
(b)	One mark for each point		5
(c)	Normal property business income basis	1	
	Rent-a-room basis	1	
	Election	1	
	Amount taxable	1	4
			31

21   QUESTION WITH HELP: PERSONAL PENSIONS

Bill, who was born on 18 August 1962, became a self employed medical consultant on 1 June 2005. Bill forecasts that he will have the following net relevant earnings from 2005/06.

	£
2005/06	25,000
2006/07	80,000
2007/08	60,000
2008/09	70,000
2009/10	75,000
2010/11	66,000
2011/12	70,000
2012/13	60,000

Bill has decided to contribute to a personal pension scheme.

Required

(a)   Calculate the maximum amount of gross pension contributions for which Bill will be entitled to tax relief in 2005/06 to 2012/13.

(b)   Explain how tax relief is given for personal pension payments.

Assume the rules in 2005/06 remain unchanged in future years.

> *If you are stuck, look at the next page for detailed help as to how you should tackle this question.*

BPP
PROFESSIONAL EDUCATION

APPROACHING THE ANSWER

For part (a), follow these steps.

Step 1   First choose a basis year for each year. The basis year can be the year concerned or any one of the five previous tax years.

Step 2   The relevant percentage depends on the taxpayer's age at the start of the tax year concerned.

21   **ANSWER TO QUESTION WITH HELP: PERSONAL PENSIONS**

(a)   Maximum contributions

Tax year	Age at start of tax year	Basis year	%	Maximum contribution £
2005/06	42	2005/06	20	5,000
2006/07	43	2006/07	20	16,000
2007/08	44	2006/07	20	16,000
2008/09	45	2006/07	20	16,000
2009/10	46	2006/07	25	20,000
2010/11	47	2006/07	25	20,000
2011/12	48	2006/07	25	20,000
2012/13	49	2009/10	25	18,750

Note. The % depends on age at **start of the tax year of contribution** not on age at the start of the basis year.

The taxpayer can choose the current year or anyone of the five previous years as his basis year. Clearly, choosing the year with the highest profits as his basis year will maximise the level of pension contributions payable.

(b)   **Personal pension contributions are paid net of basic rate tax.** This means that for a basic rate taxpayer tax relief is given at source and there is no need to take any further action.

Higher rate taxpayers obtain additional relief through their personal tax computation. The basic rate band is extended by the gross amount of the pension contribution.

22   **BERNICE BRUCE**

(a)   Bernice Bruce is single and is 47-years-old. She works as a systems analyst for a large UK resident company.

During the tax year 2005/2006 she received the following from her employers:

- A £46,000 salary.

- A £5,000 bonus on 14 February 2006. This was based on the company's accounting year ending 31 December 2005.

- The use of a petrol driven company motorcar. The car had a list price of £24,000 but the company had only paid £22,000 as part of a special group package. The CO_2 emission rate is 209 grams per kilometre. Bernice paid £4,000 towards the capital cost and contributes £10 a month towards private fuel costs.

- A stereo system which Bernice has had the use of since April 2002. The system originally cost the company £800 and it had a market value of £250 at the time it was gifted to Bernice on 6 October 2005.

In addition to the above the company paid, on behalf of Bernice, £200 a month towards the company's occupational pension scheme. Bernice does not make any contributions to the pension scheme herself.

The company has deducted a total of £15,894 income tax in respect of amounts paid to Bernice.

Bernice received the following additional income during the tax year:

- £1,350 dividends from UK companies
- £800 bank interest
- £120 building society interest

All the above figures are the amounts received or credited to the relevant accounts.

Bernice also received £100 a week throughout the year from her lodger. It is estimated that the lodger uses 10% of Bernice's household expenses, which amount to £1,800 in total for the year. The lodger has lived with Bernice for many years.

Bernice made a gift aid payment of £234 cash to Oxfam (a charity) in December 2005.

Required

(i)   Calculate Bernice's total income tax payable for the tax year 2005/2006.
                                                                    (19 marks)

(ii)   On the assumption that Bernice received her tax return from HMRC in April 2006 state the latest dates by which she should send the completed return back to HMRC if:

(a) HMRC is to calculate the tax; and
(b) Bernice is to calculate the tax   (1 mark)

(iii) State the tax implications for Bernice and the company of the pension contributions made by the company on behalf of Bernice.   (2 marks)

(b)   Christine Bull is a sole trader and has received a tax assessment from HMRC, with which she does not agree.

Required

Briefly describe the appeals procedure available to Christine if she wishes to challenge the HMRC's assessment.   (5 marks)

(c) Roberta Stagg rents a property from Paula Fish. She paid a premium of £20,000 for a 26-year lease, which started on 1 May 2005. Roberta also paid annual rent of £800 in advance on 1 May 2005. The property is used in Roberta's business, which has an accounting year end of 31 December 2005.

Required

Calculate:

(i)   the amount of property business income assessable on Paula for 2005/2006; and

(ii) the amount that Roberta may deduct from her business profits for the accounting period ending 31 December 2005.   (5 marks)

(d) Assume today's date is 22 February 2006.

Paul Hogg is 44-years-old. In the last six years he has had the following net relevant earnings (NRE).

2000/2001	£38,000
2001/2002	£39,000
2002/2003	£36,500
2003/2004	£37,000
2004/2005	£38,500
2005/2006	£38,400 (estimated)

He has never made any pension contributions

Required

(i)   Calculate the maximum amount of pension contributions Paul Hogg can pay for the tax year 2005/2006; and   (1 mark)

(ii) State how tax relief for the premiums will be given.   (2 marks)

(35 marks)

22   **ANSWER: BERNICE BRUCE**

(a) (i)   **Bernice Bruce – tax payable 2005/06**

	Non-savings income £	Savings (excl dividends) income £	Dividend income £	Total income £
Earnings (W1)	60,962			
Schedule A (W4)	950			
BI £800 × $^{100}/_{80}$		1,000		
NSB interest (gross)		150		
Dividends £1,350 × $^{100}/_{90}$			1,500	
	61,912	1,150	1,500	64,562
Less: PA	(4,895)			(4,895)
	57,017	1,150	1,500	59,667

Tax	£
£2,090 × 10%	209
£30,310 × 22%	6,668
£300 × 22% (W5)	66
£(57,017 – 32,400 – 300) = £24,317 × 40%	9,727
£1,150 × 40%	460
£1,500 × 32½%	487
Tax liability	17,617
Less: PAYE	(15,894)
BI	(200)
Dividends	(150)
Tax payable	1,373

Workings

1   Earnings

	£
Salary	46,000
Bonus (receipts basis)	5,000
Car (W2)	5,600
Fuel (W2)	4,032
Stereo (W3)	330
Pension	Exempt
Total earnings	60,962

2   Car benefit

205 – 140 = 65 ÷ 5	13%
13% + 15% =	28%

	£
List price	24,000
Less: capital contribution	(4,000)
	20,000
× 28%	5,600

Fuel benefit	
£14,400 × 28%	4,032

Partial reimbursement of fuel is not an allowable deduction.

3   Higher of:

	£
Original cost	800
Less: assessed 02/03 (20%)	(160)
assessed 03/04 (20%)	(160)
assessed 04/05 (20%)	(160)
assessed 05/06 (20%)	(80)
$(20\% \times {}^{6}/_{12})$	
	240
	£250

and MV

Total 2005/06 assessed £80 + £250 = £330

4   Either

Ordinary basis £(5,200 − 180) = £5,020

or

Rent a room £(5,200 − 4,250) = £950

ie. use rent a room £950

5   Gift aid donation

£234 × ${}^{100}/_{78}$ = £300 gross

Extends basic rate band by £300.

(ii)   Send back tax return by:

(a) **30 September 2006 if HMRC to calculate tax**
(b) **31 January 2007 if Bernice to calculate tax**

(iii)   Pension contribution

Bernice   – **no taxable benefit and not earnings for NICs.**

Company – **contributions are deductible in calculating profits subject to tax.**

(b) Christine should **appeal** to HMRC **within 30 days** of the assessment.

The appeal must **state the grounds** of the appeal.

If the appeal cannot be settled by agreement, it will be heard by the General or Special Commissioners.

There is an **appeal (on a point of law only) from the Commissioners to the High Court and then to the Court of Appeal and, finally, the House of Lords.**

(c) (i)   **Paula – Property business income 2005/06**

	£
Premium	20,000
Less: £20,000 × (26 − 1) × 2%	(10,000)
Income element of premium	10,000
Rental (accruals) ${}^{11}/_{12}$ × £800	733
Total	10,733

(ii)   **Roberta – trading expense y/e 31.12.05**

	£
Treated as rent (property business income element of premium over period of lease)	
$\dfrac{10,000}{26} \times 8/12$	256
Rent	
£800 × 8/12	533
Total deduction	789

(d)   (i)   Use highest NRE in tax year and previous 5 years

Ie. 2001/02   £39,000

Age at start of year   44

% is   20

Therefore contribution is 20% × £39,000 = £7,800

(ii)   Actual contribution is paid net of basic rate tax ie. £6,084 to give basic rate relief.

Extend basic rate by gross contribution to give additional relief.

Marking guide

	Marks	
(a) (i) BI	1	
BSI	1	
Dividends	1	
PA	½	
Tax liability	3	
PAYE/BI/dividends	2	
Workings		
Earnings – salary/bonus	1	
Car benefit	3	
Fuel benefit	1	
Stereo	2½	
Property business income	2	
Gift aid	1	19
(ii) Dates for tax return (½ mark for each exam)		1
(iii) Pension – Bernice	1	
– Company	1	2
(b) 30 days	1	
Grounds	½	
Settle by agreement	½	
Hearing before Commissioners	1	
Appeals to courts	2	5
(c) (i) Property business income	2½	
(ii) Trading expense deduction	2½	5
(d) (i) Contributions allowable	1	
(ii) Tax relief	2	3
		35

What the examiner said

'This was a [four]-part question covering several different aspects of the income tax syllabus. Part (a) required a familiar income tax calculation with the usual basic problems. In general this was answered well by most candidates, but a minority still have no idea of the different type of income and the rates to be applied to that income. This must be known and will appear in every future examination. The extension of the basic rate band was well understood, but a few candidates extended it by the net (instead of the gross) charitable payment and by the company pension contribution. It should be noted that pension contributions are either to an occupational scheme or a private pension plan and the treatment of such contributions are different in each case. Here the contribution was by the company to an occupational scheme, and therefore there is no action required in the calculation. It is an expense for the company but a tax-free benefit for the employee. Only contributions by an employee to a private pension plan are used to extend the basic rate band, contributions by an employee to an occupational scheme are deducted from salary.

The method of calculating the car benefit was well understood but many rounded the percentage up when it should be rounded down. Only a few could calculate the gift of the stereo correctly but many were aware of the rent a room relief which made much of the rental income tax-free.

Part (b) was a theory question requiring the basic appeals procedure. The Examiner was looking for mention of writing to the inspector within 30 days, appealing to the commissioners, and further redress to the courts. These simple steps would have scored five marks. There were many 'interesting' answers and marks were awarded for sensible suggestions.

Part (c) required knowledge of property business income for both rent and lease premiums. It was very encouraging to see that many candidates knew the formula for the lease premium receipt. However, few knew the deduction allowed by the payer. The major mistake in part (c) was not to restrict the deduction allowed for the payer in her accounting period (ie 8 months for the year ended 31 December 2005).

Part (d) was on pension contributions. The maximum amount of relief depends on a percentage, based on the age of the taxpayer at the start of the tax year (given in the tables provided), and the net relevant earnings for that tax year or any of the previous five years, whichever is the highest. This was generally well known. The method of obtaining relief was not clearly stated by many candidates. Basic tax relief is given at source, by payment of net premiums, and higher relief is given by extending the basic rate band.'

23   QUESTION WITH HELP: SELF ASSESSMENT

The directors, senior employees and major shareholders have approached you as chief accountant of your company, expressing confusion and anxiety concerning the system of self assessment.

Required

Prepare a statement describing the main features of the system.

> *If you are stuck, look at the next page for detailed help as to how you should tackle this question.*

APPROACHING THE ANSWER

Use this answer plan to construct your answer if you are stuck.

Step 1 When faced with a brief question requiring a written answer, it is always a good idea to read the question two or three times, to ensure that you have understood exactly what is being asked.

Step 2 Ensure that you write concisely about the main features of the self assessment system in the allotted time.

Step 3 The main features of the system concern the submission of tax returns and the payment of tax.

Step 4 You should consider the implications of the system for the company as well as for individuals.

23   ANSWER TO QUESTION WITH HELP: SELF ASSESSMENT

The main features of the self assessment system

The Return

Taxpayers must complete and submit any return issued to them **by the later** of:

(a) **31 January following the end of the tax year** which the return covers
(b) **Three months after the return was issued**

A return form includes a section for the taxpayer to compute his own tax payable (a self assessment) and this computation counts as an assessment to tax.

A taxpayer may choose not to complete the section of the return in which he works out his own tax. HMRC will then make the computation and prepare an assessment for him. However, they do not guarantee to do so in time for the taxpayer to pay the correct amount by the due date, unless the **return is submitted by the later** of:

(a) **30 September following the end of the tax year which the return covers**
(b) **Two months after it was issued**

It would be impossible for HMRC to issue return forms to every potential taxpayer every year. If no return form is issued and an individual is chargeable to income or capital gains tax, he must notify the Inspector within six months of the end of the tax year. Failure to do so can lead to a penalty equal to the tax unpaid at 31 January following the end of the tax year. However, notification is not required if a taxpayer has no chargeable gains and all of his income is dealt with under PAYE. It is also not required from taxpayers with no chargeable gains and no higher rate liability if all their income is dealt with under PAYE, is taxed at source or comprises UK dividends.

Records

Taxpayers must in general keep records until a year after the 31 January following the tax year. **Failure to keep records can lead to a penalty of up to £3,000 for each tax year affected.** However, this penalty does not apply when the only records which have not been kept are ones which could only have been needed for the purposes of claims, elections or notices not included in the return. It also does not apply where the taxpayer has not kept original vouchers for dividends and interest received net, but has kept other documents giving the same information and acceptable to the Revenue.

Enquiries

HMRC randomly select a number of returns to enquire into. They also enquire into returns where there is an identified tax risk.

Payment of Tax

The normal payment dates for income tax and Class 4 NICs for a tax year are:

(a) **31 January in the tax year,** for the first payment on account
(b) **31 July following the tax year,** for the second payment on account
(c) **31 January following the tax year,** for the final payment

For each tax year, it is necessary to compute the total income tax payable after allowing for tax deducted at source (including tax credits on dividends) and tax deducted under PAYE. Each payment on account for the next tax year is half of that amount. The payments on account for a tax year can be reduced or eliminated if the taxpayer declares, before the 31 January following the tax year, that his tax payable will be less than that for the previous tax year or will be nil. (In the former case, each payment on account is half of the reduced amount.)

Taxpayers do not need to make payments on account if:

(a)   Their income tax and NIC liability net of any tax deducted at source and tax credits on dividends for the preceding year **was less than £500,** or

(b)   **More than 80% of their income tax and NIC liability for the preceding year was met by deduction of tax at source or from tax credits on dividends.**

The final payment is the unpaid tax. There may of course be a repayment instead. The only time when the due date for the final payment is not 31 January following the tax year is when a return was not issued until after 31 October. The due date is then three months after the issue of the return.

CGT is all payable on 31 January following the tax year with no payments on account.

Employers obligations

Employers have the following obligations under the self assessment system.

(a)   To provide each employee with a **copy of his P60** by 31 May following the tax year.

(b)   To quantify taxable benefits on an **employee's P11D** and to provide the employee with a copy of his P11D by 6 July following the tax year.

(c)   To provide departing employees **with a P45 form**.

24 PENNY DONALD (06/04)

(a) Penny Donald is 46 and works as a sales manager for Modern Fashions plc, a large UK resident company. Penny's salary is £46,000 per annum.

During the tax year 2005/06 Modern Fashions plc provided Penny with the following benefits.

- The use of a company car. This was a petrol driven 2000cc BMW with a CO_2 emission level of 227 gm/km and a recommended list price of £21,000. The car was for Penny's sole use and she drove a total of 12,000 miles during 2005/06 of which 60% where on business related journeys. The company paid for all the petrol used by Penny, however Penny contributed £40 per month towards the overall cost of this.

- Workplace parking which cost the company £1,200 per year.

- Private medical insurance. This cost the company £800, but would have cost Penny £960 if she had arranged this herself.

- Childcare vouchers for nursery provision for Penny's two children. This cost the company a total of £2,520 for 36 weeks care.

- A computer system with a recommended selling price of £4,800. This Penny used at home for both business and private purposes. She estimates that 40% of the use was for business and 60% for personal use. The computer was first provided in February 2005.

Penny paid £350 per month to the company's occupational pension scheme.

Penny paid tax of £9,165 under the PAYE system for the year 2005/06.

In addition to the above Penny received the following investment income for 2005/06:

- Building society interest of £2,400
- UK dividend income of £900
- Interest of £350 from an Individual Savings Account (ISA)

The above amounts are stated as the cash amounts received.

Penny also paid a cash amount of £390 in December 2005 to the charity, Oxfam, under the gift aid scheme.

Required

Calculate the income tax payable by Penny for the tax year 2005/06.   (18 marks)

(b) Penny wishes to complete her 2005/06 tax return as soon as possible and is waiting for PAYE forms to be provided by Modern Fashions plc.

Required

(i)   State which form gives details of Penny's pay, tax and national insurance contributions for the year and by which date she should receive this.

(iii)   State which form gives details of Penny's benefits for the year and by which date she should received this.

(iii)   State by which date Penny should return her tax return for the year ended 5 April 2006 to HMRC if she wishes them to calculate the income tax due.(5 marks)

(c) Penny's husband, Adrian, also works for Modern Fashions plc and received a salary of £38,000 for 2005/06. In addition he received a car benefit calculated as £2,400 for that year. He is not a director and did not receive any bonuses.

Required

Calculate for both Adrian and Modern Fashions plc, the total national insurance contributions due for the tax year 2005/06. (5 marks)

(d) Adrian owns a house, which is not his main residence and which has been let furnished to tenants for the last four years.

The annual rent payable in advance by equal monthly instalments on the 6th of each month was £7,200 until December 2005 but was increased to £7,800 per year with effect from 6 January 2006. All amounts were received on time with the exception of that due for 6 March 2006, which was not received until 2 May 2006.

Expenditure relating to the property was as follows:

	£
Council tax	960
Water rates	380
Agent's fees	780
Re-decoration costs	1,250
New kitchen units	2,400
Mortgage interest	2,500

All these amounts were paid in 2005/06 by Adrian with the exception of the council tax which was the responsibility of the tenants.

The kitchen units were purchased to replace the existing out-dated units in an attempt to modernise the property.

The mortgage interest was paid in respect of a £50,000 interest only loan at 5% per annum.

Required

Calculate the amount of property business income for the tax year 2005/06. Assume Adrian will claim wear and tear allowance. (You are not required to calculate the amount of tax payable). (5 marks)

(33 marks)

ANSWER: PENNY DONALD

> **Tutorial note**. Take care with pension payments. Payments to an approved occupational scheme are deducted in arriving at taxable earnings. Conversely, payments to a personal pension extend the basic rate band.

(a)

	Non-savings £	Savings £	Dividends £	Total £
Salary	46,000			
Car (W1)	6,720			
Fuel (W2)	4,608			
Parking - exempt	nil			
Insurance (cost to employer)	800			
Childcare (W3)	720			
Computer (W4)	460			
	59,308			
Less: pension £350 × 12	(4,200)			
	55,108			
BSI £2,400 × 100/80		3,000		
Dividends £900 × 100/90			1,000	
STI	55,108	3,000	1,000	59,108
Less: PA	(4,895)			(4,895)
	50,213	3,000	1,000	54,213

Note: ISA interest not taxable.

Workings

(1) Car: $\dfrac{230-145}{5} = 17 + 15 = 32\%$

£21,000 × 32% = £6,720

(2) Fuel: £14,400 × 32% = £4,608

	£
(3) Childcare vouchers	2,520
Less exempt 36 × £50	(1,800)
	720

	£
(4) Computer: £4,800 × 20%	960
Less: exempt	(500)
Taxable	460

Note: Car parking at or near work is exempt.

Tax

Non-savings income

	£
£2,090 × 10%	209
£(32,400 − 2,090) = 30,310 × 22%	6,668
£500 (W5) × 22% (gift aid)	110
£(50,213 − 32,400 − 500) = 17,313 × 40%	6,925

Savings/income (excluding dividends)

£3,000 × 40%	1,200

Dividend income

£1,000 × 32.5%	325
Tax liability	15,437

		£	
Less:	PAYE	9,165	
	BSI £3,000 × 20%	600	
	Dividends £1,000 × 10%	100	(9,865)
Tax payable			5,572

Working

(5)   Gift aid $£390 \times \dfrac{100}{78} = £500$

(b) (i)   The form giving details of pay, tax and NICs is Form P60. It should be received by 31 May 2006 for the tax year 2005/06.

(ii) The form giving details of benefits is Form P11D. It should be received by 6 July 2006 for the tax year 2005/06.

(iii) Penny should submit her tax return for 2005/06 by 30 September 2006 if she wishes the Inland Revenue to calculate the income tax due.

(c) Adrian NICs

Class 1 employee

	£
£(32,760 − 4,895) = 27,865 × 11% (main)	3,065
£(38,000 − 32,760) = 5,240 × 1% (additional)	52
Total payable by Adrian	3,117

Class 1 employer

£(38,000 − 4,895) = 33,105 × 12.8%	4,237

Class 1A employer

£2,400 × 12.8%	307

Total payable by Modern Fashions plc	4,544

(d) Property business income

	£	£
Rent – April to December		
$\dfrac{9}{12} \times £7,200$		
January to March	5,400	
$\dfrac{3}{12} \times £7,800$	1,950	7,350
Expenditure		
Water rates	380	
Agents fees	780	
Re-decoration	1,250	
Interest	2,500	
Wear and tear £(7,350 – 380) × 10%	697	(5,607)
Taxable 2005/06		1,743

Notes: (1) Council tax not deductible as paid by tenants

(2) Kitchen units are capital expenditure and so not allowable

What the examiner said

This was a compulsory 33 mark question broken down into four sub parts covering different areas of income tax and national insurance contributions. This was answered very satisfactorily with many candidates scoring in the high twenties.

Part (a) required the now familiar standard income tax calculation with many of the usual basic income and expense problems. There seems to be some confusion between the calculation of a car benefit (as required here) and the use of an employee's own car and the claiming of the approved mileage allowances. Many candidates did a combination of the two, taking the 60% business usage figure as a sign to work out mileage allowances. You will not get both – where the company provides a car and petrol then you are required to work out separate benefits for the use of that car and the provision of the fuel, where the employee uses their own car and claims against the company for this usage then you are required to calculate a possible taxable benefit using the approved mileage allowances.

The other main problem here was the use of the pension and gift aid payments. Gift aid payments by individuals always require the basic rate band to be extended by the gross payment, thus allowing higher rate taxpayers to obtain an additional 18% relief for their payments. Additional care is required for pension payments as these may be to an approved occupational scheme when the treatment is to deduct the payment from the relevant employment income (as was required here) or to a personal pension plan when the treatment is the same as gift aid payments. Many candidates were confused with the pension payments but seemed to know what to do with the gift aid, although some did use the net figure instead of the gross.

Part (b) required knowledge of PAYE forms and submission dates. This area is a matter of learning facts – there is no short cut! PAYE forms and dates have and will continue to be tested in all exams.

Part (c) required knowledge of national insurance payments by an employee and his employer. Generally this was well answered with only a few confusing the rates of the self-employed with those in employment. The main problem area here was candidates calculating Class 1 insurance for the employee on the benefits – these are only subject to class 1A contributions which are payable which are payable by the company never the employee.

Part (d) required basic knowledge of the computation of property business income. Most made a reasonable attempt but many mis-read the rental income as being per month rather than annual as clearly stated. The other main points here were that the kitchen units were capital expenditure and thus should not have been deducted and the wear and tear allowance should have been 10% of rent less rates paid by the landlord – not the council tax which was paid by the tenants.

25 QUESTION WITH HELP: A COTTAGE, SHARES AND A CHATTEL

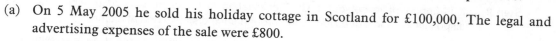

John Hammond had earnings of £18,000, dividend income of £7,200 net, paid a gift aid donation of £780 net and had the following transactions in the year ended 5 April 2006.

(a) On 5 May 2005 he sold his holiday cottage in Scotland for £100,000. The legal and advertising expenses of the sale were £800.

John had purchased the property on 5 September 1988 for £15,000 and had incurred costs of £500 on 6 June 2000 for installation of central heating and £8,000 on 1 December 2001 for the building of an extension.

The property had never been John's main residence. The indexed cost of the cottage at April 1998 was £22,500.

(b) On 14 September 2005 he sold 4,000 shares in JVD Products plc for £40,000, his previous transactions being as follows.

6 June 1988 purchased 5,000 shares cost £10,000. Indexed cost April 1998 = £15,253
12 May 2003 purchased 2,800 shares cost £12,000
12 August 2005 purchased 500 shares cost £2,000

The shares are a non-business asset for taper relief purposes.

(c) On 27 October 2005 he sold an oil painting for £7,000. Hammond had purchased the painting on 18 July 1989 for £8,000. The indexed cost of the painting at April 1998 was £11,264.

Required

Compute the income tax and capital gains tax liabilities of John Hammond for the year 2005/06.

> *If you are stuck, look at the next page for detailed help as to how you should tackle this question.*

APPROACHING THE ANSWER

Step 1   The key date to remember in any CGT question is 5 April 1998.

Step 2   It is important to set out a CGT calculation in the right way. Also, when there are several disposals as in this question, work through each disposal one at a time.

Step 3   Since all of the assets sold are investment assets (rather than business assets) non-business asset taper relief will be available for any gains arising.

Step 4   Remember that there are share matching rules.

Step 5   Losses should be set off against gains with the lowest amount of taper relief.

Step 6   When you come to work out the tax liabilities, remember that the starting and basic rate bands must be used for both income and gains. Income is dealt with first, then any gains in the starting rate band are taxed at 10%. Any gains in the basic rate band are taxed at 20%. Gains that fall in the higher rate band are taxed at 40%.

25   **ANSWER TO QUESTION WITH HELP: A COTTAGE, SHARES AND A CHATTEL**

(a)   **The cottage**

	£	£
Proceeds £(100,000 – 800)		99,200
Less: indexed cost 5.4.98	22,500	
expenditure 6.6.00	500	
expenditure 1.12.01	8,000	
		(31,000)
Gain		68,200

Non-business asset owned for eight years after 6.4.98 including the additional year.

(b)   **The disposal of shares in JVD Products plc**

Match disposals with acquisitions after 6 April 1998 on a LIFO basis:

(i)   12 August 2005 acquisition

	£
Disposal proceeds (500/4,000 × £40,000)	5,000
Less: cost	(2,000)
Gain	3,000
No taper relief	

(ii)   12 May 2003 acquisition

	£
Disposal proceeds (2,800/4,000 × £40,000)	28,000
Less: cost	(12,000)
Gain	16,000
No taper relief	

(iii)   FA 1985 pool

	£
Disposal proceeds (700/4,000 × £40,000)	7,000
Less: indexed cost (700/5,000 × £15,253)	(2,135)
Gain before taper relief	4,865

Non-business asset owned for eight years after 6.4.98 including the additional year.

(c)   **The oil painting**

	£
Proceeds	7,000
Less: cost	(8,000)
Loss (indexation allowance cannot increase)	(1,000)

(d)   **The tax liabilities**

	Non-savings £	Dividend £	Total £
Earnings	18,000		
Dividends £7,200 × 100/90	–	8,000	
STI	18,000	8,000	26,000
Less personal allowance	(4,895)		(4,895)
Taxable income	13,105	8,000	21,105

		£
Income tax on non savings income		
£2,090 × 10%		209
£11,015 × 22%		2,423
Income tax on dividend income		
£8,000 × 10%		800
Tax liability		3,432

Capital gains tax

	8 yrs taper £	Less than 3 yrs taper £
Cottage	68,200	
August 2005 shares		3,000
May 2003 shares		16,000
FA 1985 shares	4,865	
Gains	73,065	19,000
Less: loss on painting (best use)		(1,000)
Net gains before taper	73,065	18,000
Gains after taper 70%/100%	51,145	18,000
Total gains	69,145	
Less: AE	(8,500)	
Taxable gains	60,645	

Tax		£
£11,295	£(32,400 − 21,105) × 20%	2,259
£1,000	£(780 × $^{100}/_{78}$) × 20%	200
£48,350 × 40%		19,340
		21,799

Note: The basic rate is extended by the gross amount of the gift aid donation.

26   MR JOHNSON

Mr Johnson ran a very successful antiques business. He sold the business and other assets to an unconnected third party on 1 March 2006 as follows.

	Proceeds
	£
Shop	180,000
Goodwill	61,410
Fixtures	38,000
Stock	80,000
Shares in Chippo Ltd (investment company)	20,000
Antique desk	60,000
Painting	40,000

The shop and goodwill were purchased on 1 May 1993 at a cost of £40,000 and £10,000 respectively. The indexed costs at April 1998 were £46,080 and £11,520 respectively. A fixture sold for £33,000 had cost £30,000 in August 1993 (indexed cost April 1998 £34,530) and one sold for £5,000 had cost £2,000 in May 1996 (indexed cost April 1998 £2,126). The stock had been purchased for £35,000 throughout 2006.

The desk was purchased in July 1995 for £20,000 as part of trading stock. He took it for his own private residence in November 1996 when it was valued at £40,000. He did not pay any money into the shop accounts. The indexed cost of the desk at April 1998 was £42,280.

The painting was purchased in March 1982 for £18,000. The painting was never part of Mr Johnson's business assets. It had an indexed cost of £36,864 at April 1998.

Mr Johnson had inherited the shares in June 1996 when they had a probate value of £10,000. They were not a business asset for taper relief purposes. They had an indexed value of £10,630 at April 1998.

His taxable income, after personal allowances, for income tax purposes during 2005/06 amounted to £24,500.

There were no other disposals during the year and no capital losses b/fwd.

Required

(a) Calculate the capital gains tax payable by Mr Johnson for 2005/06 on the assumption that ALL the assets are sold on 1 March 2006, at the values shown.   (14 marks)

(b) Discuss the relief Mr Johnson could have claimed if he had decided to give all the assets to his daughter, rather than sell them to a third party.   (6 marks)

(20 marks)

Helping hand

Categorise assets into those chargeable to CGT and those not chargeable to CGT; and then which are business assets for taper/gift relief and those not.

116

26   ANSWER: MR JOHNSON

> **Helping hand**
>
> Chattels costing/worth less than £6,000 are exempt from CGT, as is trading stock. Personal assets (eg painting, desk) are not eligible for gift relief for a gift to an individual as they are not business assets.

(a)   CAPITAL GAINS TAX COMPUTATION

		£	£
1	**Shop**		
	Proceeds	180,000	
	Less indexed cost	(46,080)	
		133,920	
	Taper relief applies: 25% × £133,920		33,480
2	**Goodwill**		
	Proceeds	61,410	
	Less indexed cost	(11,520)	
		49,890	
	Taper relief applies: 25% × £49,890		12,472
3	**Fixtures: value > £6,000**		
	Proceeds	33,000	
	Less indexed cost (restricted)	(33,000)	
			Nil
4	**Fixtures: value < £6,000 exempt**		Nil
5	**Stock: not subject to CGT**		Nil
	Total business gains		45,952
6	**Desk**		
	Proceeds	60,000	
	Less indexed cost	(42,280)	
		17,720	
	Taper relief applies: 70% × £17,720		12,404
7	**Painting**		
	Proceeds	40,000	
	Less cost	(36,864)	
		3,136	
	Taper relief applies: 70% × £3,136		2,195
8	**Shares**		
	Sale proceeds	20,000	
	Less cost: probate value (plus indexation)	(10,630)	
	Taper relief applies: 70% × £9,370	9,370	
			6,559
	Total non business gains		21,158

	£
Total gains (£45,952 + £21,158)	67,110
Less annual exemption	(8,500)
Chargeable gains	58,610

CGT payable:

	£
(£32,400 – £24,500) = £7,900 × 20%	1,580
£(58,610 – 7,900) = £50,710 × 40%	20,284
	21,864

(b) If Mr Johnson gave his business assets to his daughter then, by means of **a joint election** by both parties, **his chargeable gains** (before taper relief) **could be reduced to nil**.

His daughter would then be deemed to acquire each asset for its market value at the date of transfer less Mr Johnson's deferred gain (before taper relief). She would use that value for purchase cost in subsequent disposal calculations.

If he gifts his **non-business assets**, however, these rules do not apply. **The market value of each asset will be deemed proceeds of sale**, so the gains in part (a) will remain unchanged.

Marking guide

		Marks
(a)	Shop, goodwill & fixtures > £6,000	$3 \times 1\frac{1}{2}$
	Fixtures < £6,000	$\frac{1}{2}$
	Stock	$\frac{1}{2}$
	Desk	$1\frac{1}{2}$
	Painting	$2\frac{1}{2}$
	Shares	$1\frac{1}{2}$
	Chargeable gains	1
	Tax payable	2
		14
(b)	1 mark per valid point	6
		20

What the examiner said

'This question produced some of the most encouraging answers. Most candidates did well and showed a sound understanding of CGT principles. Candidates should be aware that gift relief is only available on business assets – NOT personal assets.'

27   JOHN HOOD

John Hood made the following disposals of assets during the tax year 2005/06.

- 16 July 2005, 2,000 shares in ABC plc were given to his son in reward for him passing his accounting examinations. These were the only shares held by John and had cost him £3,000 on 10 September 2001. The stock exchange daily listing on 16 July 2005 showed closing prices of £4.50 and £4.90. Dealings during the day were made at £4.40, £4.50, £4.60, £4.90 and £5.00.

- 19 August 2005. An investment property was sold for £140,000. This had cost John £50,000 in June 1982. Improvements costing £16,000 were made in August 2001. Indexed cost at April 1998 was £99,250.

- 12 December 2005. A painting sold for £5,000. This had cost John £7,000 in October 1996. Indexed cost at April 1998 was £7,371.

John's income, for income tax purposes, after personal allowances, amounted to £28,500 for the year 2005/06. None of the assets were business assets for taper relief.

Required

(a) Calculate John Hood's chargeable gains for 2005/06.   (11 marks)

(b) Calculate the capital gains tax payable.   (3 marks)

(c) State when payment of the tax is due.   (1 mark)

(15 marks)

27   **ANSWER: JOHN HOOD**

(a)   **Chargeable gains 2005/06**

16.7.05

                                                        £

Market value of shares:

Lower of:

(i) $\frac{1}{4}$ of difference between upper and lower prices quoted
added to lower price ie 490p – 450p = 40p × $\frac{1}{4}$ = 10p + 450p = 460p

(ii)   Average of highest and lowest bargains made

     ie $\frac{440 + 500}{2}$ = 470p; that is 460p × 2,000   9,200

Less: cost   (3,000)

Gain   6,200

No gift relief – non business asset gifted to individual. Taper relief ownership – 10.9.01 to 16.7.05 = 3 whole years.

19.8.05

                                                        £

Proceeds   140,000

Less: indexed cost   (99,250)

             enhancement   (16,000)

Indexed gain   24,750

Taper relief ownership – 6.4.98 – 19.8.05 = 7 whole years plus additional year = 8 years

12.12.05

This disposal clearly creates a loss. The loss is restricted by using notional proceeds of £6,000.

                                                        £

'Proceeds'   6,000

Less: cost   (7,000)

Loss   (1,000)

No IA available to increase loss.

Summary

	8 years taper £	3 years taper £
Shares		6,200
Investment property	24,750	
Less: loss (best use)		(1,000)
Gains before taper relief	24,750	5,200
Taper relief 70%/95%	17,325	4,940
Total gains	22,265	
Less: annual exemption	(8,500)	
Taxable gains	13,765	

(b)   **CGT payable 2005/06**

                                                        £

£(32,400 – 28,500) = 3,900 @ 20%   780

£(13,765 – 3,900) = 9,865 @ 40%   3,946

Tax payable   4,726

(c)   **Paying tax due**

The tax is due on 31.1.07.

Marking guide

		Marks	
(a)	Valuation of shares	2	
	Cost	1	
	No gift relief	1	
	Taper relief period	1	
	Investment property gain	1	
	Taper relief period	1	
	Chattel loss	2	
	Taper relief calculation	1	
	AE	1	11
(b)	CGT payable		3
(c)	Tax due		1
			15

28   BOBBY JENKINS (06/04)

(a)   Bobby Jenkins is 44 years old and has taxable income of £29,420 (after deduction of his personal allowance) for the tax year 2005/06.

During the tax year 2005/06 Bobby disposed of the following assets:

18 May 2005: An antique vase was sold for £8,450 net of expenses of sale amounting to £550. The vase had cost £3,200 in June 2001.

21 October 2005: 2000 shares in ABC Ltd were sold for £15,400. Bobby had originally purchased 2,400 shares for £8,100 in May 2000. ABC Ltd had made a 1 for 4 rights issue for £4.50 each in September 2002. Bobby had purchased his full rights entitlement.

19 November 2005: A silver necklace was sold for £2,000. It had originally been purchased in January 2001 for £7,500 when it was thought to have originated from a much earlier period than it actually did.

2 March 2006: A watercolour painting was sold for £24,000. This had cost £8,000 in February 1986 and had an indexed cost of £13,460 in April 1998.

The shares in ABC Ltd were classed as a business asset, the other three assets were all non-business assets.

Required

Calculate the capital gains tax (CGT) payable by Bobby for the tax year 2005/06 and state when this is due for payment.   (16 marks)

(b)   Louise Duncan has for several years run a very successful business as a sole trader. During the next few months she intends to sell some of her business assets and to re-invest in other assets, some of which will have an expected useful life of 40 years and some of 70 years.

She understands that a relief may be available which would defer any capital gains that may otherwise be chargeable as a result of the above disposals and has asked you for advice.

Required

Write to Louise stating the relief available, how it affects any replacement assets and outlining the conditions which must be fulfilled for the relief to be claimed.

(Use fictitious addresses in your letter. Marks will be awarded for the style and presentation of your answer).   (12 marks)

(28 marks)

28   **ANSWER: BOBBY JENKINS**

> **Tutorial note**. Part (b) of this question required a letter to be written. It was important to write a letter as there were easy presentation marks to be gained.

(a) **Capital gains 2005/06**

Summary

	Non-business		Business
	8 years	*3 years*	*2+ years*
	£	£	£
Vase (W1)		5,000	
Shares (W2)			8,200
Painting (W3)	10,540		
	10,540	5,000	8,200
Less: loss (W4)		(1,500)	
Net gains	10,540	3,500	8,200

Note: Loss used against gain with lowest taper relief

Taper relief	70%	95%	25%
Gains after taper	7,378	3,325	2,050

	£
Total gains £(7,378 + 3,325 + 2,050)	12,753
Less: annual exemption	(8,500)
Taxable gains	4,253

Basic rate band left

£(32,400 – 29,420) = £2,980

Tax

	£
£2,980 × 20%	596
£1,273 × 40%	509
4,253	1,105

Due 31.1.07

Workings

1.   Vase

	£
Gross proceeds	9,000
Less: cost of sale	(550)
Net proceeds	8,450
Less: cost	(3,200)
Gain	5,250

Cannot exceed £(9,000 – 6,000) = 3,000 × $\frac{5}{3}$ = £5,000

Taper relief period 6.01 – 5.05 = 3 whole years.

BPP
PROFESSIONAL EDUCATION

2.   Shares

	No	Cost
		£
5.00 Acquisition	2,400	8,100
9.02 (Rights 1:4)	600	2,700
	3,000	10,800
10.05 Disposal	(2,000)	(7,200)
C/f	1,000	3,600

	£
Proceeds	15,400
Less: cost	(7,200)
Gain	8,200

Taper relief period 5.00 – 10.05 = 5 whole years

3.   Painting

	£
Proceeds	24,000
Less: indexed cost	(13,460)
Indexed gain	10,540

Taper relief period 4.98 - 3.06 = 7 whole years plus bonus year = 8 whole years

4.   Necklace

	£
Proceeds (deemed)	6,000
Less: cost	(7,500)
Loss	(1,500)

(b)

A Accountant
1 High Street
Anytown

Miss Louise Duncan
12 Broad Street
Anytown

(Date)

Dear Louise

Reliefs for replacement of business assets

Thank you for your query about the reliefs available for replacement of business assets.

As you are a sole trader, if you dispose of capital assets used in your business and gains arise, it may be possible to defer those gains. There are two different forms of relief which I will deal with in turn.

Acquisition of non-depreciating assets

This applies if you acquire another asset for use in your business which has a useful life of more than 60 years. Both the asset you are acquiring and the asset you are selling must be used in the business and be within certain categories (principally land and buildings). So, for example, if you sell a shop used in your business and buy another shop also to be used the business, these conditions will be satisfied.

The time for acquisition of the new asset is within the period which begins one year before the disposal of the original asset and three years after.

If an amount at least equal to the proceeds of the old asset is used to acquire the new asset, the whole of the gain on the old asset can be deferred. This is done by decreasing the cost of the new asset by the amount of the gain.

If an amount less than the proceeds of the old asset is invested in the new asset, the relief is restricted by the amount not invested.

Acquisition of depreciating assets

A depreciating asset is one with a useful life of 60 years or less. Fixed plant and machinery falls within this definition and is also a category of asset that qualifies for the relief.

The time limit for the investment in the new asset is the same as for non-depreciating assets.

However, in this case the gain to be deferred is not deducted from the cost of the new asset. Instead it is deferred until the earliest of:

(i)   The disposal of the new asset
(ii) The new asset ceasing to be used in the trade
(iii) 10 years from the acquisition of the new asset.

The same rules apply about the amount invested in the new asset in relation to the proceeds of the old asset.

I hope this information is helpful. Please let me know if you need any further details.

Yours sincerely

A Accountant

Marking guide

		Marks
(a)	Use of loss	1
	Taper on vase	1
	Taper on painting	1
	Taper on shares	½
	Annual exemption	½
	Tax at 20%	1
	Tax at 40%	½
	Due date	1
	Vase - original gain	1
	- marginal relief	2
	- choice	½
	Shares - pool	2
	- gain	1
	Painting	1
	Necklace	2
		16
(b)	Presentation	2
	Non-depreciating asset definition	1
	Use in business	1
	Categories	1
	Time limit	1
	Nature and amount of relief	1
	Depreciating asset definition	1
	Nature of relief	1
	Gain coming back into charge	3
		12
		28

What the examiner said. This was a two-part question on capital gains tax. Unfortunately this proves to be the poorest attempted question on every tax paper in this qualification.

Part (a) required the calculation of four separate gains including one of shares and two on chattels. To ensure a good mark candidates should learn to adopt the following procedure:

Calculate individual gains/losses
Identify any taper relief entitlement (do not action it yet)
Summarise the results at the end of the year
Use any losses against the gains with the least taper relief entitlement
Reduce the remaining gains by the taper relief
Deduct the annual exemption fro the total gains remaining
Calculate the tax due

The specific calculations in this question were:

The sale of an antique vase required the alternative calculation of the 5/3rds rule – very few candidates were aware of this and those that made an attempt were not too accurate. This is a frequently tested area of the syllabus and it is of some surprise that this is still not understood. Taper relief of 95% was applicable.

The sale of shares following a rights issue. The original purchase was made after 6 April 1998 therefore all that was required of the rights issue was it was to be added to the original purchase and effectively treated as if purchased on the same original date – giving a total purchase of 3,000 shares for a total cost of £8,200. When 2,000 are sold therefore an average cost of the shares is taken to calculate the gain. A taper relief of 25% was applicable.

The sale of a silver necklace for less than £6,000 giving a loss. This required that the proceeds be deemed to be £6,000 giving an allowable loss of £1,500. It was pleasing to note that many knew this rule. No taper relief is allowed on losses and it should have been offset against the untapered gain with the least taper relief entitlement ie the antique vase.

The sale of a pre 6 April 1998 purchased asset. The gain here should be calculated using the given indexed cost – many candidates used both the original cost and the indexed cost to give two alternative calculations. This was confusion with the pre March 1982 asset rules, which are no longer on the syllabus.

Part (b) of the question required a letter to a client explaining the rules of rollover relief. There were two easy marks for presentation – many candidates scored well on this producing sound letter formats but unfortunately most earned none on the knowledge of rollover reliefs. The revised syllabus outlined three possible reliefs that could be examined in this paper: rollover, PPR and gift relief – candidates should have been prepared for any one of these. Sadly many seemed never to have heard of rollover relief and produced very poor answers. One of the three reliefs above, whether by theory or numerical, will be tested at each sitting.

29   TERRY RABBIT

(a) Terry Rabbit, a UK resident, made the following disposals during the tax year 2005/2006:

16 May 2005

A 25% interest in a valuable piece of art. Terry had bought the piece of art on 2 August 2001, at an original cost of £200,000 and its market value immediately prior to the disposal of the 25% interest was £800,000. The 25% interest was sold for £140,000 and the remaining 75% interest retained by Terry was valued at £620,000.

14 August 2005

An antique dressing table. This had been purchased for £7,000 in May 2003 and was sold for £4,800.

18 November 2005

A house, which has been permanently let to a third party, was sold for £220,000. It had initially cost £90,000 in March 1982 and an extension had been added in August 2001 at a cost of £20,000. The indexed cost of the house in April 1998 was £184,320.

Required

Calculate Terry's total chargeable gains (before the annual exemption) for the tax year 2005/2006.   (11 marks)

(b) Hilary Swan owns and currently lives in a property, which has been her only and main residence for several years. She is now about to sell the property and is aware that the disposal of a person's main residence is usually exempt from a charge to capital gains tax. Unfortunately Hilary has had periods of absence from the property either because of work or lengthy visits to relations and is worried that these may affect her exemption from the capital gains charge.

Required

State the FOUR occasions when periods of absence are deemed to be periods of actual occupation and therefore will not affect her exemption.   (4 marks)

(c) (i)   State the FOUR main conditions that have to be met in order that a sole trader can claim rollover relief for the purposes of capital gains tax.

(ii) State when the amount of rollover relief may be restricted.   (5 marks)

(20 marks)

29   ANSWER: TERRY RABBIT

(a)   **Summary – Capital Gains 2005/06**

	3 year taper £	8 year taper £
Interest in art work (W1)	103,158	
House		15,680
Less: loss (W2)	(1,000)	
Gains before taper relief	102,158	15,680
Taper relief 95%/70%	97,050	10,976
Total gains 2005/06 (before AE)	108,026	

Note: The loss is set against the gain which attracts the least amount of taper relief (ie where the highest percentage of the gain remains taxable).

Workings

1	Art work	£
	Proceeds	140,000
	Less: cost	

$$£200,000 \times \frac{140,000}{140,000 + 620,000} \qquad (36,842)$$

	Gain	103,158

Taper relief period 2.8.01 to 16.5.05 = 3 whole years.

2	Dressing table	£
	Deemed proceeds	6,000
	Less cost	(7,000)
	Allowable loss	(1,000)

3	House	£
	Proceeds	220,000
	Less: indexed cost	(184,320)
	Extension	(20,000)
	Indexed gain	15,680

Taper relief period 6.4.98 to 5.4.05 = 7 whole years plus additional year = 8 years.

(b)   **Four periods of deemed occupation**

(i)   Absence for any reason up to 3 years (eg visiting relations)

(ii)   Absence for employment abroad

(iii)   Absence for work where Hilary was required to live elsewhere up to 4 years

(iv)   Last 3 years of ownership

(c)   (i)   **Four main conditions for sole trader to claim rollover relief**

1   Old and new assets used in trade of person claiming relief

2   Old and new assets fall within one (but not necessarily the same one) of the classes of asset qualifying for relief

3   New asset acquired within the period beginning one year before and three years after the disposal of the old asset

4   New asset brought into use in trade on its acquisition

(ii)   Rollover relief is restricted if an amount less than the proceeds of the old asset is invested in the new asset.

Marking guide

			Marks	
(a)	*Artwork*:			
	Proceeds		½	
	Cost – part disposal		2	
	Taper relief period		½	
	Table			
	Deemed proceeds		1	
	Cost		½	
	House			
	Proceeds		½	
	Indexed cost		1	
	Extension		½	
	Taper relief period		½	
	Summary			
	Set off loss correctly		1	
	Taper – 95%		1	
	Taper – 70%		1	
	Total gains (before AE)		1	11
(b)	One mark for each point			4
(c)	One mark for each point			5
				20

What the examiner said

'This was a capital gains tax question requiring calculations of basic gains and theory knowledge of both principal private residence (PPR) and rollover reliefs. The calculations of the gains were of a good standard with many knowing the part disposal formula and the restriction of loss relief for chattels.

The two theory areas, the deemed occupation rules for PPR and the rollover relief conditions, were not so well-answered. Both these areas required rote learning of simple facts and no amount of guesswork helped. Previous reports have stressed the importance of theory knowledge. This question illustrated the need for it and showed candidates had not studied the entire syllabus.'

30   TOMMY COLEBROOK (PILOT PAPER)

(a)   Tommy Colebrook earned £28,480 taxable income (after deduction of his personal allowance) in the tax year 2005/06.

During the same year he disposed of several capital assets as follows.

14 May 2005: four acres of land were sold for £240,000. They have been part of a larger plot of twelve acres, which had been purchased on 2 May 2001 for £360,000. Auctioneer's fees of 2% were payable on the sale proceeds. The market value of the remaining eight acres in May 2005 was £400,000.

17 August 2005: a vintage motor car, which he had purchased in June 2002 for £39,000 was sold for £48,000.

14 December 2005: an antique desk that had cost £3,500 in September 1994 was sold for £9,009 net of 1% auctioneers fees. The indexed value of the desk in April 1998 was £3,916.

6 February 2006: a painting, which had cost £42,000 in May 2002, was sold for £9,500 after it was discovered it was not an original.

None of the assets had been used in a business.

Required

Calculate the capital gains tax (CGT) payable by Tommy for the tax year 2005/06 and to state the date when it is due.

(14 marks)

(b)   Angus McPherson is a successful businessman running a chain of butcher's shops in Scotland. His son, Archie, is also a qualified butcher. On the occasion of Archie's 25th birthday Angus gave him one of the freehold shops.

The shop had cost Angus £80,000 in October 1994 and has an indexed value of £89,600 in April 1998. The market value at the date of the gift in September 2005 was £142,000.

In addition to the shop Angus gave Archie a painting by a renowned local artist entitled 'Scottish Bulls'. This had cost Angus £1,200 in May 2002 and was worth £10,400 at the time of the gift in September 2005.

Required

Calculate the chargeable gains of Angus for the tax year 2005/06 assuming that any reliefs available are claimed.

Your answer should include details of who must make a claim for the available relief(s) and by when it must be done.

(8 marks)

(22 marks)

Helping hand. When a question is in two parts like this you will maximise your chance of passing if you allocate your time carefully between the two parts.

---

30   ANSWER: TOMMY COLEBROOK

(a)   **Land**

	£
Proceeds	240,000
Less: Auctioneers fees	(4,800)
Less: Cost £360,000 × $\dfrac{240,000}{240,000 + 400,000}$	(135,000)
Gain before taper relief	<u>100,200</u>

The land was held for four complete years, so 90% of the gain will remain chargeable after taper relief.

Car

Motor cars are exempt assets so no gain or loss arises on the disposal of the vintage car.

Desk

	£
Proceeds	9,009
Less: Indexed cost	(3,916)
Gain before taper relief	<u>5,093</u>

The gain cannot exceed $(£9,009 \times \dfrac{100}{99} - 6,000) \times 5/3 = \underline{£5,167}$

∴ The lower gain of £5,093 is taken.

The desk has been owned for 8 years for taper relief purposes (7 years plus the additional year), so 70% of the gain will remain chargeable after taper relief.

Painting

	£
Proceeds	9,500
Cost	(42,000)
Loss	<u>(32,500)</u>

The loss should be set against the gain that attracts the least taper relief (ie where the highest amount of the gain remains chargeable).

	£	£
Gain on land	100,200	
Less: Loss	(32,500)	
	<u>67,700</u>	
After taper relief (90%)		60,930
Gain on desk after taper relief (70%)		3,565
		64,495
Less: Annual exemption		(8,200)
Net gains		<u>55,995</u>

CGT

	£
£3,920 (W) × 20%	784
£52,075 × 40%	20,830
<u>£55,995</u>	<u>21,614</u>

CGT of £21,614 is payable on 31 January 2007.

Working

Remaining basic rate band:

	£
Basic rate band	32,400
Taxable income	(28,480)
	3,920

(b)

	£
Deemed proceeds (market value)	142,000
Less: Indexed cost	(89,600)
	52,400
Less: Gift relief	(52,400)
Chargeable gain	Nil

A claim for gift relief must be made jointly by Angus and Archie by 31 January 2012 (ie 5 years after the 31 January following the tax year in which the disposal occurred).

Painting

	£
Deemed proceeds	10,400
Less: Cost	(1,200)
Gain before taper relief	9,200

Maximum gain

$5/3(10,400 - 6,000) = £7,333$

Lower gain taken $= £7,333$

Gain after taper relief $(95\%) = £6,966$

It is not possible to claim gift relief on the gift of the painting as the painting is not a business asset.

Marking guide		Marks
(a)	*Gain on land*	
	Fees	1
	Cost	2
	Taper relief	½
	Car – exempt	1½
	Desk	
	Gain before taper	½
	Maximum gain	1
	Taper relief	½
	Painting	
	Loss	1
	Offset loss	1
	Annual exemption	1
	Gain after taper relief	1
	Tax payable	2
	Due date	1
		14
(b)	Gain on shop	2½
	Gain on painting	2
	Taper relief	½
	Gift relief	1
	Claim/due date	2
		8
		22

31 AMANDA PERKINS (12/04)

(a) Amanda Perkins is 29 years old and is a UK resident. During the tax year 2005/06 she made the following disposals of capital assets.

18 August 2005: Four acres of land were sold for a gross amount of £80,000. An auctioneer's fees of 10% was charged on the disposal. The land had been part of a ten-acre plot that had cost £120,000, in September 2001. The market value of the remaining six acres was £240,000, in August 2005. The land has never been used as a business asset.

15 November 2005: A house, which had never been her main residence, was sold for £290,000. It had cost £100,000 in May 1985 and had an indexed cost of £186,000 on 6 April 1998.

14 January 2006: 2000 shares in APC Ltd were sold for £3,500. Amanda's purchases of APC Ltd shares have been:

14 September 1993	1,000 shares for £500
16 November 2002	500 shares for £550
19 October 2005	500 shares for £775
20 January 2006	200 shares for £300

The indexed value of the FA 1985 pool on 6 April 1998 was £640.

The shares are classed as a business asset.

Amanda had a capital loss of £8,500 brought forward as at 6 April 2005.

Required:

Calculate Amanda's net taxable gains for the tax year 2005/06.

(You are not required to calculate the capital gains tax payable.)   (16 marks)

(b) Amanda's father, Harry, owns a small shop, which he has always used as a business asset. It cost him £90,000 in October 2001.

On 14 February 2006 he sold the shop to Amanda for £115,000 when it had a market value of £185,000.

Required:

(i) Calculate Harry's chargeable gain on the disposal of the shop assuming that holdover relief is claimed on the gift of the business asset.   (4 marks)

(ii) State Amanda's base cost for future capital gains tax purposes.   (1 mark)

(21 marks)

31   ANSWER: AMANDA PERKINS

Tutorial Note. Off-set of capital losses is a popular exam topic as students forget to deduct the loss before applying the relevant taper relief to each asset and then deducting the annual exemption from total gains. Capital losses should be off-set against the asset with the highest taper relief percentage (i.e. 100% and 95%) first to maximise the tax saving.

(a)   **Amanda Perkins**
      Net taxable gains

	£
Land – part disposal	
Proceeds	80,000
Less: auctioneer's fees	(8,000)
	72,000

$$\text{Less:} \quad \text{cost} \times \frac{A}{A+B}$$

$$120,000 \times \frac{80,000}{80,000 + 240,000}$$

	£
Gain before taper relief	(30,000)
	42,000

The land was held for 3 complete years, so 95% of the gain will remain chargeable after taper relief.

House (not main residence)	£
Proceeds	290,000
Less: indexed cost	(186,000)
Gain before taper relief	104,000

The house has been owned for 8 years for taper relief purposes (7 years plus the bonus year), so 70% of the gain will remain chargeable after taper relief.

Shares

Match disposal with shares bought in next 30 days

January 2006

	£
Proceeds $(\frac{200}{2,000} \times £3,500)$	350
Less: cost	(300)
Gain	50

No taper relief.

Match disposal with shares bought after 6 April 1998 on a LIFO basis

October 2005

	£
Proceeds $(\frac{500}{2,000} \times £3,500)$	875
Less: cost	(775)
Gain	100

No taper relief.

November 2002

	£
Proceeds $(\frac{500}{2,000} \times £3,500)$	875
Less: cost	(550)
Gain before taper relief	325

Shares have been owned for 3 complete years therefore 25% of the gain will remain chargeable after taper relief.

Match disposal with shares bought after 31 March 1982 but before April 1998 (ie in FA 1985 pool)

	£
Proceeds ($\frac{800}{2,000} \times £3,500$)	1,400
Less: Indexed cost (W1)	(512)
Gain before taper relief	888

Shares have been owned for 7 years since taper relief introduced in April 1998 therefore 25% of the gain will remain chargeable after taper relief.

Working

1   *FA 1985 pool*

	No	Cost	Indexed cost
	£	£	£
6.4.98	1,000	500	640
Disposal	(800)	(400)	(512)
c/f	200	100	128

Loss offset

% chargeable after taper relief	100%	95%	70%	25%	Total
	£	£	£	£	£
Land		42,000			
House			104,000		
Shares – Jan 05	50				
Shares – Oct 05	100				
Shares – Nov 02				325	
Shares – FA85 pool				888	
	150	42,000	104,000	1,213	
Less: capital loss b/f (**note**)	(150)	(8,350)			
	Nil	33,650	104,000	1,213	
		× 95%	× 70%	× 25%	
Gain after taper relief		31,967	72,800	303	
Total gains					105,070
Less: annual exemption					(8,500)
Net taxable gains					96,570

Note. Capital loss offset against assets with the highest taper relief percentage (ie largest amount remaining chargeable after taper relief) first to maximise tax saving.

(b) (i)   **Harry Perkins**
         Chargeable gain

	£
Proceeds: market value	185,000
Less: cost	(90,000)
Gain	95,000
Less: gift relief (*balancing figure*)	(70,000)
Gain left in charge (cash received – original cost) £(115,000 – 90,000)	25,000
Taper relief (business asset, 4 years, 25% × £25,000)	6,250

(b) (ii)   **Amanda's base cost**

	£
Market value	185,000
Less: gift relief	(70,000)
	115,000

Marking scheme

				Marks
(a)	Land:	auctioneer's fee		1
		cost of part disposal		2
		95% taper relief		½
	House:	indexed gain		1
		70% taper relief		½
	Shares:	next 30 days: Jan '06		1½
		since 6.4.98: Oct '05		1
		since 6.4.98: Nov '02		1½
		FA 85 pool		2
	Offset of capital loss b/f			2
	Taper relief			2
	Annual exemption			1
				—
				16
(b)	(i)	Gain		1
		Gift relief		2
		Taper relief		1
	(ii)	Base cost		1
				—
				5
				21

What the examiner said

'This was a two-part question on capital gains tax. Once again candidates struggled on this area with only a few demonstrating sound knowledge.

Part (a) of the question required the calculation of gains resulting from three separate disposals. The first involved a part disposal and despite this being tested on numerous occasions many were still not able to calculate the part disposal cost. This is a standard calculation and will be frequently tested in the future.

The second disposal was the sale of an assert purchased before 6 April 1998. The new syllabus guidelines clearly states that in these situations the indexed cost at 6 April 1998 will be given and therefore the calculation of the gain merely requires that this cost be deducted from the sale process – the original cost figure is not required.

The third disposal was shares. This produced all sorts of inventive solutions! Where an individual makes a series of purchases of shares in the same company when these shares are sold they must be identified in the correct order. The pooling of shares stopped on 5 April 1998 for individuals but many candidates pooled all the shares together and had one average cost for the disposal and one calculation. The correct answer involved four separate calculations, one for each of the separate holdings.

The final point was to use the capital loss brought forward against the gains with the least taper relief entitlement first before actually tapering the gains and then using the annual exemption.

Part (b) involved restricted gift relief. Very few candidates were able to calculate this properly. Given that this is one of only three areas that could be tested in this part it was expected that more candidates should have been able to calculate the chargeable gain and the amount to be heldover. Where a business asset is gifted that gain is calculated using the full market value as proceeds, and the resulting gain heldover against the base cost of the new owner. If actual proceeds exceed the original cost (as was the case here) this amount is chargeable immediately and only the balance of the gain can be heldover.'

141

32   BOX PLC

Box plc makes up accounts to 31 March each year. In its 12-month period ending 31 March 2006 it has the following transactions in capital assets.

26 May 2005

20,000 shares in Crate plc sold for £124,000. These shares had been purchased as follows.

26 May 1992	13,000 shares for	£24,000
24 October 2000	5,000 shares for	£27,500
22 May 2005	2,000 shares for	£12,000

(7 marks)

21 August 2005

A painting, which had been hanging in the managing director's office, was sold for £5,800. It had been purchased for £8,000 in October 1998.

(2 marks)

12 January 2006

Four acres of land from a large plot of 12 acres were sold for £380,000. The 12 acres had been purchased in March 1985 for £450,000. The remaining eight acres had a market value of £950,000 on 12 January 2006.

(4 marks)

14 February 2006

A factory was sold for £250,000 (gross) at auction. The auctioneer charged a fee of 10% of selling price. The factory had originally been purchased in July 1989 for £80,000 plus purchase costs of £5,000. It had been extended at a cost of £20,000 in June 1998.   (4 marks)

Required

Calculate the total chargeable gain for Box plc for the year ending 31 March 2006.

(17 marks)

Assume indexation factors

May 1992 – October 2000	0.232
October 2000 – May 2005	0.108
March 1985 – January 2006	1.067
July 1989 – February 2006	0.662
June 1998 – February 2006	0.175

32 **ANSWER: BOX PLC**

Box plc: Chargeable gains y/e 31.3.2006

Summary of gains and losses

	£
Shares: last nine days (W1)	400
Shares: FA 1985 pool (W2)	48,369
Land (W3)	114,244
Factory (W4)	60,230
	223,243
Less: painting (W5)	(2,000)
Net chargeable gains	221,243

Workings

1   *Crate Ltd shares - acquisition in last nine days*

	£
Proceeds 2,000/20,000 × £124,000	12,400
Less: cost	(12,000)
Gain	400

Acquisitions matched with disposals under the 9 day rule never enter the FA 1998 pool.

2   *Crate Ltd shares - FA 1985 pool*

	No.	Cost £	Indexed cost £
26.5.92			
Acquisition	13,000	24,000	24,000
24.10.00			
IA			
0.232 × £24,000			5,568
			29,568
Acquisition	5,000	27,500	27,500
c/f	18,000	51,500	57,068
26.5.05			
IA			
0.108 × £57,068			6,163
			63,231
Disposal	(18,000)	(51,500)	(63,231)
c/f	nil	nil	Nil

Gain

	£
Proceeds 18,000/20,000 × £124,000	111,600
Less: cost	(51,500)
Unindexed gain	60,100
Less indexation allowance	
£(63,231 – 51,500)	(11,731)
Indexed gain	48,369

3   *Land*

	£
Proceeds	380,000
Less: cost	
$\dfrac{380}{380+950} \times £450,000$	(128,571)
Unindexed gain	251,429
Less: indexation allowance (1.067 × £128,571)	(137,185)
Indexed gain	114,244

4   *Factory*

		£
Gross proceeds		250,000
Less: costs of disposal		(25,000)
Net proceeds		225,000
Less: cost (including costs of acquisition)		(85,000)
enhancement		(20,000)
Unindexed gain		120,000
Less: indexation allowance on cost (0.662 × £85,000)		(56,270)
indexation allowance on enhancement (0.175 × £20,000)		(3,500)
Indexed gain		60,230

5   *Painting*

	£
Proceeds (deemed)	6,000
Less: cost	(8,000)
Loss	(2,000)

Marking guide   **Marks**

Shares: matching	1
Last 9 days	1½
FA 1985 pool	3½
Total gain	1
Land	4
Factory	4
Painting	2
	17

What the examiner said

'This question involved a company disposing of shares and other capital items. The calculations of gains on the shares was a complete mystery to most. Few realised that the shares had to be classified into different holdings ie less than 10 days old and the 1985 pool. The disposal took place on a LIFO basis.'

33   QUESTION WITH HELP: ABEL LTD AND CANE LTD

(a)   Abel Ltd, a UK trading company with no associated companies, produced the following results for the year ended 31 March 2006.

	£
Income	
Adjusted trading profit	243,000
Rental income	15,000
Bank deposit interest accrued (non-trading investment)	5,000
Capital gains: 25 September 2005	35,000
28 March 2006	7,000
(There were capital losses of £8,000 brought forward at 1 April 2005)	
Patent royalty accrued (relates to trade: received gross, not included above)	1,000
Dividends from UK companies (including notional tax credits – June 2005)	15,000
Charges paid	
Gift aid donation	7,000

Required

(i)   Compute the corporation tax payable by Abel Ltd for the above accounting period.

(ii)   Advise the directors of the effect on the company's tax liability of their decision to sell the above asset on 28 March 2006.

(b)   Cane Ltd, a UK trading company with no associated companies, produced the following results for the year ended 31 March 2006.

	£
Income	
Adjusted trading profit	33,000
Bank deposit interest (non-trading investment)	1,000
Capital gain	4,000

The company paid a dividend of £25,000 to its five shareholders (all individuals) on 28 February 2006.

Required

Compute the corporation tax payable by Cane Ltd for the above accounting period.

If you are stuck look at the next page for detailed help as to how you should tackle this question.

APPROACHING THE ANSWER

Part (a)

Step 1   In working out a company's profits chargeable to corporation tax (PCTCT), we must bring together all taxable profits, including gains. You must therefore start by drawing up a working, and picking out from the question all relevant profit figures.

Step 2   Once you have found the PCTCT, you can consider the rate of tax. You should find that SCR marginal relief applies. If you do not, look carefully to see whether you have missed anything.

Step 3   Having completed your computation, you should move on to part (ii). The answer will become clear if you remember that everyone would like to pay less tax, and to pay their tax later.

Part (b)

Step 1   Again, work out the company's PCTCT. Does it fall below the upper threshold for starting rate marginal relief?

Step 2   Consider the effect of the dividend paid to the non-corporate shareholders.

Step 3   Why do you need to work out the underlying rate of CT?

33   ANSWER TO QUESTION WITH HELP: ABEL LTD AND CANE LTD

(a) (i)   CORPORATION TAX COMPUTATION

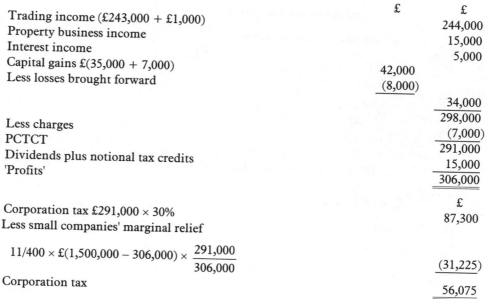

	£	£
Trading income (£243,000 + £1,000)		244,000
Property business income		15,000
Interest income		5,000
Capital gains £(35,000 + 7,000)	42,000	
Less losses brought forward	(8,000)	
		34,000
		298,000
Less charges		(7,000)
PCTCT		291,000
Dividends plus notional tax credits		15,000
'Profits'		306,000

	£
Corporation tax £291,000 × 30%	87,300
Less small companies' marginal relief	
$11/400 \times £(1,500,000 - 306,000) \times \dfrac{291,000}{306,000}$	(31,225)
Corporation tax	56,075

Notes

1   Gift aid donations are always paid gross.

2   As the patent royalty received related to the trade it is included within trading income.

(ii)   The disposal on 28 March 2006 increased the profits for small companies rate purposes from £299,000 to £306,000, thus leading to the application of the full rate less small companies marginal relief. If the disposal had not been made, the mainstream corporation tax would have been only £284,000 × 19% = £53,960, a saving of £2,115. It might be that had the disposal taken place in the next accounting period, starting only four days later, the gain would only have been taxed at 19% (assuming FY 2005 rates continue to apply), giving rise to tax of £1,330. Thus the company might have been able to save tax of £2,115 – £1,330 = £785 (and this ignores the benefit of an extra month's indexation allowance). Payment of tax on the gain would also have been deferred by 12 months.

(b) CORPORATION TAX COMPUTATION

	£
Trading income	33,000
Interest income	1,000
Capital gain	4,000
PCTCT	38,000

This falls below the starting rate marginal relief upper threshold and so the rate of tax will be less than 19%. Therefore, the rules on additional tax relating to distributions to non-corporate shareholders apply.

Work out CT using normal rules:

	£
£38,000 × 19%	7,220

Less: starting rate marginal relief

$$£(50,000 - 38,000) = 12,000 \times \frac{19}{400}$$ (570)

CT   6,650

Underlying rate is

$$\frac{6,650}{38,000} \times 100 = 17.5\%$$

CT payable is   £

£25,000 (dividends) × 19%   4,750

£(38,000 − 25,000) = £13,000 × 17.5%   2,275

Total CT payable   7,025

34   UK FABRICS (12/04)

UK Fabrics Ltd has no associated companies and has previously drawn up its accounts to 31 December each year. During 2005 the company decided to change its permanent accounting year end to 31 March.

The following information is provided in respect of the 15 month period of account ending 31 March 2006.

	£	£
Turnover		3,410,000
Cost of sales		(1,600,000)
Gross profit		1,810,000
Profit on sale of an asset (note 1)		141,000
Rent received (note 2)		168,000
Depreciation	70,000	
Wages	320,000	
Utility costs	48,000	
Increase in general provision for bad debts	18,000	
Miscellaneous expenses (note 3)	28,000	
		(484,000)
Net profit		1,635,000

Notes

1   The profit shown is the gain, after accounting for depreciation, on the sale of an unwanted showroom for £273,510 in August 2005. The showroom had originally been purchased for £210,000 in October 2001. The indexation factor for October 2001 to August 2005 is 0.095.

2   The rent received is in respect of an office block leased to another UK resident company for £12,000 per month. The unpaid amount is due in April 2006.

3   The amount of £28,000 comprises:

	£
Legal fees in respect of trade debt collection	5,000
Customer entertainment	2,000
Gifts of food hampers to customer valued at £60 each	3,000
Legal fees in respect of the renewal of a 40 year lease on its factory	3,500
Office expenses (all allowable)	14,500
	28,000

4   The tax written down value of plant and machinery qualifying for capital allowances as at 1 January 2005 was £280,000. During the 15 months ending 31 March 2006 the company purchased a machine for £40,000 on 14 May 2005 and a car (which is not a low emission car) for £9,000 on 2 February 2006. An old machine, which had previously cost £5,000 in May 2004, was sold for £4,000 on 14 August 2005. The company is classed as medium sized for capital allowances purposes.

Required:

For each of the two tax accounting periods comprising UK Fabric's fifteen month period of account ending 31 March 2006:

(a)   Calculate the maximum capital allowances available.   (5 marks)

(b)   Calculate the trading income (after capital allowances).   (6 marks)

(c)   Calculate the corporation tax payable.   (8 marks)

(19 marks)

34   **ANSWER: UK FABRICS**

> **Tutorial Note.** For a 15 month long period of account, one adjustment to profits is required for the whole period of account. The amounts added back and deducted are those appearing in the 15 month set of accounts. The total adjusted profit is then time apportioned 12:3 into 2 columns. The results of the two capital allowance workings feed in to a column each.
>
> In a written answer it is important to use headings and sub-headings based on the requirement to maximise your marks. This ensures you answer the question set (& follow instructions about what information is not required such as details of deregistration).
>
> 2 presentation marks for a letter are still achievable, even if you don't know anything about the requirement, by including the client's & firm's address, date, reference and signing off correctly.

(a)   **Capital allowances – 1 January 2005 to 31 December 2005**

	FYA	General pool £	Total allowances £
TWDV b/f		280,000	
Additions – machine	40,000		
Disposals – old machine		(4,000)	
	40,000	276,000	
WDA @ 25% pa		(69,000)	69,000
FYA @ 40%	(16,000)		16,000
		24,000	
TWDV c/f		231,000	85,000

Capital allowances – 1 January 2006 to 31 March 2006

	General pool £	Total allowances £
TWDV b/f	231,000	
Additions – car	9,000	
	240,000	
WDA @ 25% × 3/12	(15,000)	15,000
TWDV c/f	225,000	

(b)   **Trading income**

	£	£
Net profit per accounts		1,635,000
Add back:		
Depreciation	70,000	
Increase in general provision	18,000	
Miscellaneous expenses:		
Customer entertainment	2,000	
Gifts of food hampers	3,000	
		93,000
Deduct:		
Profit on sale of asset	(141,000)	
Rent received (per accounts)	(168,000)	
		(309,000)
Adjusted trading profits		1,419,000

Notes

1   Legal fees for trade debt collection are allowable expenses because they are incurred wholly and exclusively for the purposes of the trade.

2 Legal fees on renewal of short (ie ≤ 50 years) lease are allowable expenses.

	year ended 31 Dec '05 £	3 mth period ended 31 Mar '06 £
Adjusted profit (£1,419,000 × 12/15 × 3/15)	1,135,200	283,800
Less: CAs (from part (a)(i))	(85,000)	(15,000)
Trading income	1,050,200	268,800

(c) **Corporation tax payable**

	year ended 31 Dec '05 £	3 mth ended 31 Mar '06 £
Trading income	1,050,200	268,800
Property business income (accruals) (£12,000 × 12/3)	144,000	36,000
Capital gain (W1)	43,560	
PCTCT	1,237,760	304,800
Add: FII	-	-
'Profits'	1,237,760	304,800

SCR limits

Lower	300,000	3/12	75,000
Upper	1,500,000	3/12	375,000

Therefore SCR marginal relief applies in both cases.

Tax liability	£	£
£1,237,760/£304,800 × 30%	371,328	91,440
Less: marginal relief		
11/400 (1,500,000 – 1,237,760)	(7,212)	
11/400 (375,000 – 304,800)		(1,930)
	364,116	89,510

(W1) Capital gain	£
Proceeds	273,510
Cost	(210,000)
	63,510
IA (0.095 × £210,000)	(19,950)
	43,560

Marking guide

Marks

(a) Disposal of old machine – proceeds limited to cost   1
    25% WDA   1
    40% FYA on new machine   1
    Purchase of car (no FYA)   ½
    25% WDA × 3/12   1½

(b) Add back: Depreciation   ½
             Increase in bad debt provision   ½
             Entertainment of customers   ½
             Gifts of food hampers   ½
    Deduct: Profit on sale of asset   ½
             Rental income (per accounts)   ½
    Note: no adjustment required for:
        - legal fees on renewal of short lease   ½
        - legal fees for trade debt collection   ½
    Split of adjusted profit 12:3   1
    Deduction of CAs from part (a)(i)   1

(c) Property business income on accruals basis   2
    Chargeable gain   2
    Tax liability
    y/e 31 December 05: 30% - MR   1½
    adjusted limits: 3/12   1
    p/e 31 March 2006: 30% - MR   1½

<u>19</u>

What the examiner said

'This particular question involved a long period of account for both capital allowances and the calculation of tax. Few candidates attempted this well and most had no idea that a period in excess of twelve months must be split into two separate chargeable periods of the first twelve months and the balance (in this case 3 months). This results in two separate tax bills – there is no such thing as a 15-month tax bill!

The capital allowance calculation was particularly disappointing as this area is tested in nearly every paper. Common mistakes involved:

* Not splitting the period into two
* not prorating the WDA for the 3-month period
* Giving FYA for the car
* Treating the cheap car as a separate 'pool'
* Taking the sale proceeds as £5,000 instead of the lower of original cost and the actual sale proceeds of £4,000

Part (b) required the accounting profit to be adjusted. Those that had an idea that the period should be split actually split too early and adjusted in two parts – the adjustment process is done as one long period and then prorated after. Other mistakes included:

* Adjusting for the unpaid rent (this only done when assessing the property business income figure)
* Adding back income and deducting expenses (the reverse to what is required!)
* Adjusting for every figure and hoping that something must be correct!

Part (c) required the calculation of tax for the two separate periods. This was very poorly answered. Encouragingly many candidates calculate the gain on the showroom disposal correctly although a few applied the indexation factor to the gross gain rather than the original cost.

The most common errors were:

- only doing one calculation
- Not applying the accruals basis on the rent and thus omitting the arrears
- Not apportioning the rat thresholds for the 3-month period
- Not being able to use the marginal relief formula given in the rate and allowances table.'

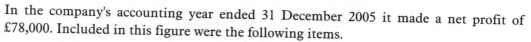

35   DANDY PLC (PILOT PAPER)

(a)   Dandy plc is a UK resident company with two, 60% owned, subsidiaries.

In the company's accounting year ended 31 December 2005 it made a net profit of £78,000. Included in this figure were the following items.

Income

(i)   £4,500 dividend from a UK company in which it owns 40% of the shares.

(ii)   £6,300 dividends from each of the two 60% owned subsidiaries.

(iii)   £20,000 insurance proceeds in respect of lost profit as a result of the temporary closure of its factory.

(iv)   £8,000 rent. The annual amount due is £9,000 and the tenant has promised to pay the balance in January 2006.

(v)   £10,000 debenture interest in respect of £250,000 debentures issued at 4% per annum.

Expenditure

(i)   £8,000 interest. This is in respect of a £180,000 loan borrowed in 2004 at 5% pa interest. The borrowed money was used to buy the factory in which Dandy plc now conducts its business. The outstanding amount will be paid in January 2006.

(ii)   £6,000 interest. This is in respect of a £120,000 loan borrowed in 2003 at 5% pa interest. The borrowed money was used to buy a factory which is now being let to a third party.

(iii)   £3,000 to Oxfam under the gift aid scheme.

(iv)   £1,000 fees in respect of an issue of ordinary shares.

(v)   £400 overdraft interest.

(vi)   £235,000 wages. Of this £20,000 was in respect of an employee seconded to one of its subsidiaries and £15,000 in respect of an employee seconded to a UK national charity. The balance was in respect of employees employed at its UK head office.

(vii)   £9,000 patent royalties. These are directly related to the company's main products.

(viii)   £11,000 depreciation.

(ix)   £8,000 entertainment. Of this £3,000 was in respect of employees and £5,000 in respect of overseas customers.

In addition to this, and **not** included in the accounts, the company had a chargeable capital gain of £9,000 in the year and a capital loss brought forward of £3,000 on 1 January 2005.

The company claimed capital allowances of £16,000.

Required

For Dandy plc for the year ended 31 December 2005:

(i)   Calculate the adjusted trading income.   (9 marks)
(ii)   Calculate the corporation tax payable.   (8 marks)
(iii)   State the date of payment.   (1 mark)

(b) Dandy plc's Value Added Tax (VAT) quarter ended 31 December 2005 Dandy plc had the following transactions.

	£
Standard rated sales	80,000
Zero-rated sales	30,000
Standard rates purchases	45,000

The above amounts are all inclusive of VAT where applicable.

In addition the company purchased plant and machinery in November 2005 for £18,000 exclusive of VAT.

Bad debts of £5,000 (exclusive of VAT) were written off in the period. Of this £3,000 was originally due on 15 January 2005 and £2,000 on 14 September 2005.

Required

Calculate the amount of VAT owed to Dandy plc for the VAT quarter ended 31 December 2005.

(4 marks)

(22 marks)

Helping hand. It is important to distinguish between interest due on a loan taken out for trading purposes and interest due on a loan taken out for non trade purposes. The former is dealt with under trading income. The latter under miscellaneous income.

---

35   ANSWER: DANDY PLC

(a) (i)   **Trading income**

	£
Net profit per accounts	78,000
Less	
Dividend income (£4,500 + £6,300 + £6,300)	(17,100)
Rent	(8,000)
Debenture interest	(10,000)
Interest accrual (Note 1) (£180,000 × 5% – 8,000)	(1,000)
Capital allowances	(16,000)
Add	
Interest (Note 2)	6,000
Gift Aid donation	3,000
Fees re share issue	1,000
Employee seconded to subsidiary (Note 3)	20,000
Depreciation	11,000
Entertaining – customers	5,000
Trading income	71,900

Notes

1   As the interest arose on a trading loan relationship the accrued amount can be deducted in computing trading income.

2   The interest on the loan used to buy a factory which is let to a third party is interest on a non trading loan relationship. This means that it must be added back in computing trading income.

3   The cost of secondment to a charity is allowable.

(ii)

	£
Trading income	71,900
Property business income	9,000
Interest income (£10,000 – £6,000)	4,000
Net chargeable gain (£9,000 – £3,000)	6,000
	90,900
Less: Gift aid donation	(3,000)
	87,900
Add: FII (£4,500 × 100/90)	5,000
'Profits'	92,900

Note. Only FII received from companies who are not 51% subsidiaries is included within the calculation of 'profits' for small companies' rate purposes.

FY04 and FY05

£87,900 × 19% (W)   £16,701

Working: Tax rate

'Profits' are below the small companies' lower limit of £100,000 (£300,000/3) and above the starting rate upper limit of $\frac{£50,000}{3}$ =£16,667, so the small companies rate of tax applies. This is 19% in FY04 and FY05.

(iii) **£16,701 is due for payment on 1 October 2006.**

(b)

	£
Standard rated sales (£80,000 × 7/47)	11,915
Less:	
Standard rated purchases (£45,000 × 7/47)	(6,702)
Plant (£18,000 × 17½ %)	(3,150)
Bad debts (£3,000 × 17½ %)	(525)
VAT due	1,538

Note

The Input VAT on bad debts can only be reclaimed when the bad debt is over six months old.

Marking guide   **Marks**

  (a)   *Deductions*

(i)	Dividend income	1	
	Rent	½	
	Debenture interest	½	
	Interest accrual	1	
	Capital allowances	½	
	Additions		
	Interest	½	
	Gift aid donation	½	
	Fees re share issue	1	
	Employee seconded to subsidiary	1	
	Depreciation	½	
	Entertaining	1	
	Items requiring no adjustment	1	
			9
(ii)	Trading income	½	
	Property business income	1	
	Interest income	1	
	Net chargeable gain	1½	
	Gift aid donation	1	
	FII	1	
	Corporation tax	2	
			8
(iii)	Due date for payment of CT	1	

  (b)   *VAT on*

	Sales	1	
	Purchases	1	
	Plant	1	
	Bad debts	1	
			4
			22

---

36   CON LTD

Con Ltd is a small UK trading company with an accounting year-end of 31 March. The following transactions in plant took place in the year ending 31 March 2006:

Purchases

15 May 2005	A second hand machine	£5,000
14 June 2005	A new machine	£12,500
17 August 2005	A new car	£10,000

Disposals

| 12 June 2005 | A machine (original cost £3,500) | £4,000 |

In addition to the above, a car which had cost £18,000 some years ago was traded in for a new car. The trade in value of the old car was £6,000 and additional cash of £9,000 was paid for the new car. The new car is not a low emission vehicle.

The tax written down values brought forward as at 1 April 2005 were:

| Plant and machinery | £16,000 |
| Expensive car | £8,500 |

On 1 September 2005 the company purchased a second hand factory for £80,000. This had cost the original purchaser £100,000 on 1 September 1995 and had always been used for a qualifying purpose. Con Ltd immediately used the factory for a qualifying purpose.

Con Ltd had purchased its current factory (which is still used for a qualifying purpose) in August 2000 for a total cost of £190,000. This cost had been made up as follows:

Land	£55,000
Tunnelling	£10,000
Solicitor's fees	£5,000
Showroom	£35,000
Factory	£85,000

Required

Calculate the maximum capital allowances that can be claimed by Con Ltd for its accounting period ending 31 March 2006.   **(17 marks)**

> **Helping hand**. When a second hand building is purchased you must write off the lower of the purchase price and the original cost over the remaining tax life of the building.

36   **ANSWER: CON LTD**

Con Ltd - Capital Allowances y/e 31 March 2006

Plant and machinery

	FYA £	Pool £	Car (1) £	Car (2) £	CAs £
TWDV b/f		16,000	8,500		
Additions not with FYAs		10,000		15,000	
		26,000			
Disposals		(3,500)	(6,000)		
		22,500			
BA			2,500		2,500
WDA @25%		(5,625)		(3,000) max	8,625
		16,875			
Additions	17,500				
FYA @ 40%	(7,000)				7,000
		10,500			
TWDV c/f		27,375		12,000	
CAs					18,125

New factory

As Con Ltd is the second owner, it will write off the lower of the original cost (£100,000) or its own cost (£80,000) ie. £80,000.

The tax life of the building is 25 years from 1.9.1995. 15 years of the tax life remain.

The allowance for y/e 31.3.06 is therefore:

$$\frac{£80,000}{15} = \underline{£5,333}$$

Original factory

Qualifying expenditure was:

	£
Tunnelling	10,000
Factory	85,000
	95,000

The cost of the land is not qualifying. The solicitor's fees do not relate to the construction of the building and so are not allowable. The showroom is a non-qualifying part exceeding more than 25% of the expenditure so must be excluded.

The allowance for y/e 31.3.06 is:

£95,000 x 4% = £3,800

Total allowances are therefore:

£(18,125 + 5,333 + 3,800) = £27,258

Marking guide

		Marks
General pool	3	
Car (1)	2	
Car (2)	2	
FYA	2	
		9
Secondhand factory	2	
New factory: qualifying expenditure	4	
IBA	1	
Total allowances	1	
		8
		17

What the examiner said

'This was standard capital allowances question involving mainly plant and machinery but also industrial buildings. The plant and machinery calculation was done well by many candidates but a few managed to confuse gains and allowances together, especially on the disposal of the two items of plant. Where a car is traded in for another then there are essentially two transactions, one on the sale of the old car for the trade in value and then the second is the purchase of the new car for the trade in value plus the cash settlement, very few candidates knew this. The calculation of the buildings caused many problems. Second hand buildings do not get 4% WDA but require a calculation of the residue of expenditure spread over the remaining tax life. This should have been an easy two marks if candidates knew this formula, sadly very few did.

The allowances for the new buildings were, thankfully, calculated better. However even here candidates still lost easy marks by including the land in the calculation – land never qualifies for industrial buildings allowance. It was pleasing that many knew the 25% rule for the showroom and showed their workings to demonstrate why it should be omitted.'

37   BAKER PRODUCTIONS PLC (06/04)

Baker Productions plc owns 60% of Street Industries Ltd and 40% of Holmes Ltd. All three companies are UK resident and make up their accounts to 31 March annually.

During its accounting year ended 31 March 2006 Baker Productions plc had the following items of income and expenditure:

Income:

	£
Adjusted trading profit (before capital allowances)	262,400
Rent	24,000
Bank interest	8,000
Debenture interest	14,000
Dividend from Street Industries Ltd	9,000
Dividend from Holmes Ltd	5,400

Expenditure:

Gift aid donation to the charity, Oxfam	2,000

Baker Production plc had purchased its factory premises on 1 May 2000 for £140,000 from another UK company, which had purchased the factory new on 1 August 1997 for £100,000. Both companies have always used the factory for qualifying industrial purposes.

Baker Productions plc had balances brought forward as at 1 April 2005 on its plant and machinery pool and a short life asset (SLA) of £112,000 and £2,900 respectively. The only transactions affecting these amounts were the disposal of the SLA on 2 September 2005 for £3,400 and the purchase of a second-hand machine for £20,000 on 1 December 2005. The SLA sold had originally cost £6,000 in May 2003. The company is classed as medium sized for capital allowances purposes and always claims the maximum possible allowances.

In addition to the above Baker Productions plc sold an office complex, which had never been used in the business, for £180,000 in December 2005. This had originally cost £60,000 in August 1987 and had been extended at a cost of £21,000 in May 1995.

A trading loss of £10,849 and a capital loss of £10,500 were brought forward as at 1 April 2005.

Required

(a)   Calculate the total capital allowances for plant and machinery and the total industrial buildings allowances (IBA) for Baker Productions plc in respect of the year ended 31 March 2006;

(6 marks)

(b)   Calculate the corporation tax payable by Baker Productions plc for the year ended 31 March 2006.

(13 marks)

Indexation factors

August 1987 – December 2005	0.877
May 1995 – December 2005	0.281

(19 marks)

37   ANSWER: BAKER PRODUCTIONS PLC

> **Tutorial note**. It is important to learn a standard layout for the corporation tax computation.

(a)   **Capital allowances year ending 31.3.06**

Plant and Machinery

	FYA £	Pool £	SLA £	Allowances £
TWDV b/f		112,000	2,900	
Disposal			(3,400)	
BC			(500)	(500)
WDA @ 25%		(28,000)		28,000
		84,000		
Addition	20,000			
FYA @ 40%	(8,000)	12,000		8,000
TWDV c/f		96,000		
Allowances				35,500

Industrial Building Allowance

2nd hand building

Lower of   original cost (1) £100,000
              purchase price (2) £140,000

ie £100,000

Tax life ends on 1.8.97 + 25 = 1.8.22

Date of purchase 1.5.00

Unexpired life 22 years 3 months

Allowance year ending 31.3.06

$$\frac{100,000}{22.25} = £4,494$$

Total allowances £(35,500 + 4,494) = £39,994

(ii)   **Corporation tax year ending 31.3.06**

	£	£
Adjusted trading profit	262,400	
Less: capital allowances	(39,994)	222,406
Less: trading loss b/f		(10,849)
Trading income		211,557
Property business income		24,000
Interest income (8,000 + 14,000)		22,000
Capital gain (W)	40,479	
Less: capital loss b/f	(10,500)	29,979
		287,536
Less: gift aid donation		(2,000)
PCTCT		285,536
Add: dividend from Holmes Ltd (N) £5,400 × $\frac{100}{90}$		6,000
'Profits'		291,536

Note: Dividend from Street Industries Ltd is not included because it is from 51% or more subsidiary.

Working

Capital gain	£
Proceeds	180,000
Less: cost	(60,000)
extension	(21,000)
Unindexed gain	99,000
Less: indexation on cost	
0.877 × £60,000	(52,620)
Indexation on enhancement	
0.281 × £21,000	(5,901)
Indexed cost	40,479

Number of associated companies = 2 (Baker, Street)

Holmes Ltd is not associated because Baker Productions plc does not own over 50% of the shares.

SCR thresholds

Upper $\dfrac{£1,500,000}{2} = £750,000$

Lower $\dfrac{£300,000}{2} = £150,000$

SCR marginal rate relief applies

	£
£285,536 × 30%	85,661
Less: marginal rate relief	
$£(750,000 - 291,536) = 458,464 \times \dfrac{285,536}{291,536} \times \dfrac{11}{400}$	(12,348)
CT payable	73,313

Marking guide

			Marks
(a)	SLA disposal and BC		
	WDA 1½		
	Purchase and FYA		½
	IBA 1		
		3	6
(b)	Trading profit		½
	CAs ½		
	Loss b/f		1
	Property Business Income		½
	Interest Income		1
	Capital gain		2½
	Loss b/f		1
	Gift aid		1
	Dividend from Holmes Ltd		1
	Dividend from Street Industries Ltd		1
	SCR thresholds		1
	Tax @ 30%		1
	Marginal rate relief		1
			13

What the examiner said

Part (a) was on capital allowances for both plant and machinery and a second hand building. The plant and machinery calculation was attempted well but many confused the balancing charge by calling it a balancing allowance. Where a 'de-pooled' asset is sold for more than its tax written down value then a negative figure will appear in the column. This results in a balancing charge which is then either added to profits or netted off against other capital allowances.

The calculation of the industrial buildings allowance was not done well. Many simply used 4% or went back over the history of the asset and calculated all sorts of allowances – using methods never seen before! The simple calculation required here is to take the lower of the original cost and the new purchase price and divide that by the remaining tax life. This gives you an annual written down allowance to be used against profits. The remaining tax life is the life left after the latest purchase date (1 May 2000) until the end of twenty five years starting from the date the asset was originally taken into use (1 August 1997). This must be measured in exact months not round years.

Part (b) was a standard corporation tax assessment for 13 marks. Marks can be gained or lost by putting or not putting items in the correct place of the assessment. A standard layout must be learnt, for instance trading losses b/forward must be deducted from trading profit and capital losses must be deducted from capital gains – many candidates were not awarded marks because these losses were used against incorrect items. Some candidates still confuse capital allowances and capital gains – these are two totally different things. Capital allowances replace depreciation and is therefore an adjustment against profits whereas capital gains are 'profits' on the disposal of assets and is a separate taxable income figure in the assessment.

Understanding of the effects of associated companies is new to the syllabus and was required here. The number of associated companies affects the tax thresholds. Associate companies are those where the holding is in excess of 50% - therefore the 40% holding in Holmes does not make this an associate. The tax thresholds are therefore divided by two not three giving upper limits of £150,000 and £750,000. In addition to this dividends received from associated companies are not used in the tax calculation anywhere therefore only the dividend from Holmes should have been included in the profits definition.

Some candidates mistakenly calculated the gain by using taper relief and an annual exemption – these two items only apply to individuals never to companies.

38   QUESTION WITH HELP: CARRYING BACK A LOSS

Galbraith Ltd is a company resident in the United Kingdom making garments for sale to the tourist industry at its factory in Callander. It started to trade on 1 April 2003. The company's results for the first three years are as follows.

	Year ended 31 March		
	2004	*2005*	*2006*
	£	£	£
Trading profit/(loss) (as adjusted for taxation)	125,000	(697,000)	80,000
Bank interest accrued (non-trading investment)	263,000	185,000	24,000
Chargeable gains	60,360	0	3,000
Dividends received from UK companies (net) (January)	6,000	3,000	3,750
Gift aid donations paid (gross)	40,000	57,000	30,000

Required

(a) Calculate the corporation tax liabilities for the three years after claiming maximum loss relief at the earliest possible times.

(b) In respect of the mainstream corporation tax for the accounting period ended 31 March 2006, state when this will be due for payment and state the filing date.

> *If you are stuck, look at the next page for detailed help as to how you should tackle this question.*

APPROACHING THE ANSWER

Step 1 In requirement (a) you are alerted to the likelihood of encountering losses. First, set out the figures for trading profits and leave space for losses carried forward under s 393(1) ICTA 1988.

Step 2 Set out the remainder of the profits subject to tax and then deduct losses from the total. Questions usually require loss relief to be claimed as quickly as possible. Remember that s 393A(1) ICTA 1988 requires losses to be set off first against total profits of the loss-making accounting period. Only after these have been extinguished can losses be carried back. Any remaining losses are carried forward, but may only be set against trading profits (not total profits). Remember that losses are set off before gift aid donations, so gift aid donations may become unrelieved.

Step 3 Remember that certain companies pay corporation tax at the starting rate. Does it apply in this case?

Step 4 Remember that certain companies are required to pay for their anticipated corporation tax liability by quarterly instalments. Does this apply to Galbraith Ltd?

38   ANSWER TO QUESTION WITH HELP: CARRYING BACK A LOSS

(a)

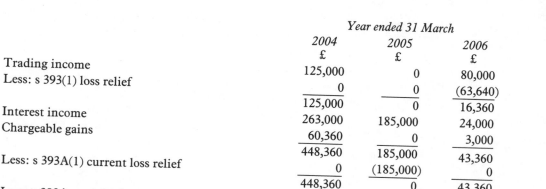

	Year ended 31 March		
	2004	2005	2006
	£	£	£
Trading income	125,000	0	80,000
Less: s 393(1) loss relief	0	0	(63,640)
	125,000	0	16,360
Interest income	263,000	185,000	24,000
Chargeable gains	60,360	0	3,000
	448,360	185,000	43,360
Less: s 393A(1) current loss relief	0	(185,000)	0
	448,360	0	43,360
Less: s 393A carry back	(448,360)	0	0
	0	0	43,360
Less: gift aid donation	0	0	(30,000)
Profits chargeable to corporation tax	0	0	13,360
Unrelieved gift aid donation	£40,000	£57,000	

The loss carried forward at 1 April 2006 is £(697,000 – 185,000 – 448,360) = £63,640.

There is no corporation tax liability for either of the first two years.

For the third year, the position is as follows.

Profits chargeable to corporation tax = £13,360.

'Profits' = £13,360 + (£3,750 × 100/90) = £17,527. As 'profits' are between the starting rate upper and lower limits of £50,000 and £10,000 respectively, starting rate marginal relief applies.

	£
Corporation tax	
£13,360 × 19%	2,538
Less: starting rate marginal relief	
$(£50,000 - £17,527) \times \dfrac{13,360}{17,527} \times {}^{19}/_{400}$	(1,176)
	1,362

(b)   The due date for payment of the £1,362 corporation tax for the year to 31 March 2006 is 1 January 2007. The filing date is 31 March 2007. **Galbraith Ltd is not required to pay its anticipated corporation tax liability in quarterly instalments as it does not pay corporation tax at the full rate.**

39   BALTIC PLC

(a)   Baltic plc is a UK trading company making up accounts to 31 March each year. Following poor results the company ceased to trade on 31 March 2005. The most recent sets of accounts showed the following details.

	2003 £	2004 £	2005 £	2006 £
Trading profits	40,000	30,000	20,000	
Trading loss				(69,000)
Property business income	4,000	4,000	4,000	4,000
Chargeable gain		6,000		
Allowable capital loss			(7,000)	
Gift aid donation	500	500	500	500

Required

(i)   Calculate the profits chargeable to corporation tax (PCTCT) for all the years concerned after maximum relief is claimed for the loss made in the year ended 31 March 2006.   (8 marks)

(ii)   Identify the amounts that will be unrelieved after all claims have been made.

(2 marks)

(b)   Pacific plc has always made up accounts to 31 December annually. During the year to 31 December 2005 the trading accounts showed a net profit of £850,000. Included in these accounts were the following items.

Payments

(i)   Entertainment of £4,000, of this amount £2,500 was on customers and the remainder was spent on the company's own staff.

(ii)   Repairs of £25,000. This amount included a figure of £20,000 to repair a warehouse, which was purchased in August 2005. The warehouse had been badly damaged a fire before Pacific plc had purchased it. The repair was necessary to put the warehouse into a usable condition. The remaining £5,000 was spent on general office repairs.

(iii)   Patent registration fee of £2,000.

(iv)   Debenture interest of £8,000. This represents interest on £100,000 of 9% debentures issued to fund the purchase of plant and machinery used in the business.

Receipts

(v)   Insurance proceeds of £40,000 in respect of a claim for lost profits whilst the factory was closed by a minor flood.

(vi)   £14,000 representing the profit on the sale of a packing machine sold in September. The machine had been purchased in 2002 and had been used in the business since that date.

Required

Explain the action required, if any, to adjust the trading profits of Pacific plc for tax purposes because of the items listed above. Your answer should clearly state your reasons for the action you are proposing and whether you will be adding back, deducting or leaving the relevant figure unadjusted.

Note you are not required to calculate the actual final profit figures.   (12 marks)

(22 marks)

Helping hand

In part (b) you are required to clearly state your reasons for the action you are proposing. If you do not do this you cannot hope to pass the question.

---

39   ANSWER: BALTIC PLC

(a) (i)   BALTIC PLC

Year ended 31 March

	2003 £	2004 £	2005 £	2006 £
Trading income	40,000	30,000	20,000	0
Property business income	4,000	4,000	4,000	4,000
Chargeable gains	0	6,000	0	0
	44,000	40,000	24,000	4,000
Less: s.393A current period	0	0	0	(4,000)
	44,000	40,000	24,000	0
Less: s.393A carry back	(1,000)	(40,000)	(24,000)	0
	43,000	0	0	0
Less: gift aid donation	(500)	0	0	0
PCTCT	42,500	0	0	0
Unrelieved gift aid		500	500	500

S393A(1) loss memorandum

	£
Loss incurred in y/e 31.3.06	69,000
Less: s.393A(1): y/e 31.3.06	(4,000)
y/e 31.3.05	(24,000)
y/e 31.3.04	(40,000)
y/e 31.3.03	(1,000)
Loss remaining	0

(ii)   The capital loss of £7,000 is unrelieved because it cannot be carried back.

The gift aid donations of 3 × £500 = £1,500 are also unrelieved.

Note: On cessation of a trade a loss can be carried back for 36 months.

(b)   PACIFIC PLC

Item	Treatment	Explanation
Entertaining customers	Add back £2,500	Not allowable
Entertaining staff	Leave £1,500	Allowable
Repairs to warehouse	Add back £20,000	Disallowable capital expenditure as incurred to put asset into fit state for use (*Law Shipping* case)
General office repairs	Leave £5,000	Allowable revenue expenditure
Patent registration fee	Leave £2,000	Allowable
Debenture interest	Leave £8,000 Deduct £1,000 being the additional amount of interest due	Interest accrued on loan for trading purposes is allowable
Insurance proceeds for loss of income	Leave £40,000	Compensation received in one lump sum for the loss of income is likely to be treated as income (*Donald Fisher(Ealing)Ltd v Spencer*)
Profit on sale of machine	Deduct £14,000	Dealt with under CAs and capital gains

Marking guide

			Marks
(a)	(i)	Trading income	1½
		Property business income	2
		Capital gain	½
		s393A current	1
		s393A c/b	1½
		Gift aid	½
		PCTCT	1
			8
	(ii)	Capital loss	1
		Unrelieved gift aid	1
			2
			10
(b)	2 marks for each payment/receipt (including explanation)		12
			22

What the examiner said

'This was a corporation tax question covering two completely separate areas of loss relief and trading income adjustments. Part (a) on loss relief was poorly answered but part (b) saw many candidates attempting it with a degree of understanding.

Part (a) on loss relief saw many candidates merely copy the information from the question paper answer booklet. This did score limited marks but unless the candidate made some attempt to use relief then few marks could be gained. There seemed to be a common approach by overseas candidates – lump all four years together and get one overall total – a strange tactic! The secret here was to adopt a columnar format.

Part (b) of the question was a theory question requiring candidates to describe the action necessary to adjust trading profits to give adjusted trading profits. This was well attempted by most candidates and markers were lenient in the exact interpretation of stated actions. Candidates are advised that in future they should read the question carefully and answer what is required. The question clearly states that the items were included in the profit and loss and candidates had to explain any actions required to adjust profits giving reasons and stating whether adding back, subtracting or no action was required. Fewer marks were earned than could have been because candidates did not do as requested.'

40   COMPANIES

(a)   A company is only charged to UK corporation tax on its total profits if it is UK resident.

Required

State the two tests that HMRC will use to see if a company is UK resident.

(3 marks)

(b)   The following items of expenditure were made by a limited company, which satisfies the definition of a small sized company under the Companies Acts, during its 12 months accounting period ending 31 March 2006.

Note. there were no tax written down values brought forward.

–   16 April 2005 – £80,000 spent on a retail shop in a large city centre.

–   14 August 2005 – £147,000 spent on a new factory. It was taken into immediate industrial use, and the cost consisted of:

	£
Land	20,000
Structure	80,000
Architect fees	5,000
Drawing office	10,000
Administration office	32,000
	147,000

–   1 September 2005 - £140,000 on a second-hand factory. The original owner had paid £110,000 to the constructor for the factory on 1 September 1987, it was brought into use on that day. The factory is to be, and always has been, used for an industrial purpose.

–   19 October 2005 – £15,000 spent on thermal insulation to its factories.

–   31 January 2006 – £18,000 on a new car to be used by the company's managing director of which 50% of the use will be private.

–   28 February 2006 – £40,000 spent on plant and machinery.

Required

Calculate the total amount of capital allowances available to the company for its accounting period ending 31 March 2006.   (13 marks)

(c)   A UK resident company, makes a trading loss of £20,000 in its accounting period ending 31 December 2005.

Required

Explain the way in which the company may utilise this loss and state by when the claims have to be made.   (7 marks)

(23 marks)

40 ANSWER: COMPANIES

(a) **Tests of company UK residence**

The two tests HMRC will use are:

(i) A company **incorporated in the UK is resident in the UK for tax purposes.**

(ii) A company not incorporated in the UK **is resident in the UK** for tax purposes if **its central management and control is in the UK.**

(b) **Capital allowances y/e 31.3.06**

16.4.05 No allowances due. Retail shop not industrial building.

14.8.05 Industrial building

Land cost – not allowable

Drawing office – industrial building (*IRC v Lambhill Ironworks Ltd* (1950))

Administration offices – not allowable as more than 25% of total cost £(147,000 – 20,000 = 127,000 × 25% = £31,750).

Full WDA given for accounting period as factory in use at end of period. Allowance is £(80,000 + 5,000 + 10,000) is £95,000 × 4% = £3,800

1.9.05 Industrial buildings allowance will be given on the lower of:

(i) original cost;

(ii) cost to buyer.

ie original cost – £110,000.

Tax life of building ends on 1.9.87 + 25 years = 1.9.2012

Unexpired life 1.9.05 – 1.9.2012 is 7 years.

WDA for y/e 31.3.06 is therefore $\frac{£110,000}{7} = £15,714$.

19.10.05 Thermal insulation is deemed plant and machinery (see below).

31.1.06 Expensive car. No adjustment for private use for company. Calculation below – no FYA.

28.2.06 Plant and machinery – see below.

	FYA £	Pool £	Expensive car £	Allowances £
19.10.05				
Insulation	15,000			
Less: FYA @ 40%	(6,000)	9,000		6,000
31.1.06				
Car			18,000	
Less: WDA @ 25%			Max (3,000)	3,000
28.2.06				
Plant and machinery	40,000			
Less: FYA @ 40%	(16,000)	24,000		16,000
TWDA's c/f		33,000	15,000	
Allowances given				25,000

Summary of allowances

	£
Factory 1	3,800
Factory 2	15,714
Plant and machinery /car	25,000
Total allowances y/e 31.3.06	44,514

(c) **Loss reliefs**

    (i)   **Set-off loss against current profits.**

        These are total profits before deducting gift aid donations.
        Claim within two years of end of accounting period in which loss arose.

    (ii)   **Set-off loss against profit of an accounting period falling wholly or partly within the 12 months of the start of the period in which the loss was incurred.**

        'Profits' are total profits before deducting gift aid donations.
        Claim as in (i)

    (iii)   **Carry forward against future profits of the same trade.**

        No claim is required.

Marking guide

			Marks	
(a)	UK incorporation		1	
	Central management		2	3
(b)	Retail shop		1	
	Industrial building – new factory		3	
	Industrial building – 2nd hand factory		2	
	Thermal insulation		1	
	Expensive car		2	
	FYAs		2	
	WDA		1	
	Summary		1	13
(c)	Set off v current profits		3	
	c/b loss		2	
	c/f loss		2	7
				23

What the examiner said

'This involved three separate areas of corporation tax.

Firstly, the two tests for residence status. Very few candidates scored many marks on this and confused it with the residence rules of individuals. Marks were awarded for the mention of incorporation in the UK and control in the UK.

Secondly, knowledge on capital allowances. This was very poorly answered. Many answers confused the rules on industrial buildings and plant and machinery. The rules are totally different and must not be mixed. This is vital knowledge for both sole traders and companies and all tax textbooks would give good coverage of the differences. Candidates had obviously not read them. Even the rates table supplied with the paper gives clues by giving the rates to be used for both categories – this was obviously overlooked by most.

The third part of the question involved the rules of company loss relief. Again, many confused the rules of sole traders and companies. Although the rules are similar they are not the same. Many expressed the relief available in terms of sole traders quoting sections 380 and 385 from ICTA 1988 when what was required were sections 393A(1) and 393(1). However marks were awarded for mentioning how it was to be used and against what type of income despite the wrong section numbers being quoted. Only a few knew that the claim had to be made within 2 years of the end of the accounting period containing the loss.'

41 HADDIT PLC

(a) Haddit plc is a UK resident trading company that has experienced a downturn in its trade in recent years. As a result the company ceased trading on 31 October 2005.

The company's results during recent years have been:

	Year to 30 Jun 02	*6 months to 31 Dec 02*	*Year to 31 Dec 03*	*Year to 31 Dec 04*	*10 months to 31 Oct 05*
	£	£	£	£	£
Trading profit/(loss)	40,000	18,000	14,000	10,000	(98,000)
Interest income	4,000	2,000	2,000	1,000	2,000
Chargeable gain/loss	(3,000)	4,000	Nil	(2,000)	Nil
Property business income	5,000	5,000	5,000	5,000	5,000
Gift Aid	(3,000)	(3,000)	(2,000)	(1,000)	(1,000)

Required:

Calculate the profit chargeable to corporation tax (PCTCT) for each of the periods concerned on the assumption that Haddit plc will claim the maximum reliefs available.

(9 marks)

(Note: you are not required to calculate the amount of corporation tax due)

(b) Cargo Ltd is a small UK resident trading company.

In its 15-month accounting period to 31 March 2006 the company had the following transactions in fixed assets:

Purchases:	16 May 2005	Second-hand plant	£24,000
	14 June 2005	New plant	£98,500
	18 August 2005	A car for a director's use	£26,000
	19 December 2005	A car for general business use	£11,000
	14 February 2006	New plant	£85,000
Sales:	17 July 2005	Plant (original cost £48,000)	£18,000
	20 August 2005	A car (original cost £18,000)	£7,000
	2 March 2006	A short life asset (SLA)	£4,000

Notes:

• The car purchased on 19 December 2005 was classed as a low emission car (CO_2 emission rate less than 120 grams per kilometre).

• The car purchased on 18 August 2005 was used 20% for business and 80% privately.

• The SLA was purchased in September 2003 for £9,000.

In addition to the above the company had traded in an old car for a newer model in November 2005. The old car had cost £11,000 in January 2003 and had a trade in value of £3,000. The company paid an additional £6,000 cash for the new model. This car, which is not a low emission car, is used 100% for business purposes.

The balance of the pools as at 1 January 2005 were:

Plant and Machinery	£248,000
Expensive car	£9,000
Short life asset (SLA)	£4,200

Required

Calculate the minimum capital allowances available to Cargo Ltd for the period(s) ending 31 March 2006.

(11 marks)

(20 marks)

Helping hand. Split the long period of account into two accounting periods and calculate capital allowances separately for each period. The first accounting period is 12 months long.

---

41   ANSWER: HADDIT PLC

(a) **Haddit plc**

	Y/e 30.6.02	6 months to 31.12.02	Y/e 31.12.03	Y/e 31.12.04	10 months to 31.10.05
	£	£	£	£	£
Trading income	40,000	18,000	14,000	10,000	0
Interest income	4,000	2,000	2,000	1,000	2,000
Gains	0	1,000 (N1)	0	0	0
Property business income	5,000	5,000	5,000	5,000	5,000
	49,000	26,000	21,000	16,000	7,000
Less: s393A current period	0	0	0	0	(7,000)
	49,000	26,000	21,000	16,000	0
Less: s393A carryback	(24,500) (N2)	(26,000)	(21,000)	(16,000)	0
	24,500	0	0	0	0
Less: gift aid	(3,000)	0	0	0	0
PCTCT	21,500	0	0	0	0
Unrelieved gift aid		3,000	2,000	1,000	1,000

Loss memorandum

	£
Loss incurred p/e 31.10.05	98,000
Less: used 31.10.05	(7,000)
used 31.12.04	(16,000)
used 31.12.03	(21,000)
used 31.12.02	(26,000)
used 30.6.02	(24,500)
Loss unrelieved	3,500

Notes

1   Capital losses

Loss in y/e 30.6.02 c/f to set against gain in p/e 31.12.02

Loss in y/e 31.12.04 unrelieved

2   Terminal loss

Loss relief available to c/b 36 months

Only 6 months of y/e 30.6.02 falls within this period so only $^{6}/_{12} \times £49,000 = £24,500$ can be relieved.

Helping hand. Did you read the question carefully? You were specifically told not to calculate the amount of corporation tax due and you would have only wasted time by doing so.

(b) **Cargo Ltd**

	FYA £	Pool £	Exp. Car (1) £	SLA £	Exp. Car (2) £	Allowances £
y/e 31.12.05						
TWDVs b/f		248,000	9,000	4,200		
Additions – no FYA		9,000			26,000	
		257,000	9,000	4,200	26,000	
Disposals						
(18,000 + 3,000)		(21,000)	(7,000)			
		236,000	2,000	4,200	26,000	
BA (N)			(2,000)			2,000
WDA @ 25%		(59,000)		(1,050)	(3,000)	63,050
		177,000		3,150	23,000	
P+M						
(24,000 + 98,500)	122,500					
Less: FYA @ 40%	(49,000)	73,500				49,000
Low emission car	11,000					
Less: FYA @ 100%	(11,000)	nil				11,000
TWDV c/f		250,500		3,150	23,000	
Allowances						125,050
P/e 31.3.06						
Disposal				(4,000)		
				(850)		
BC				850		(850)
WDA @ 25% × $^3/_{12}$		(15,656)			(750)	16,406
P+M	85,000					
Less: FYA @ 40%	(34,000)					34,000
		51,000				
TWDV c/f		285,844			22,250	
Allowances						49,556

Notes

1. No restriction for private use for company.

2. WDAS are time apportioned in a short accounting period. FYAs are not.

Marking guide

			Marks	
(a)	Trading income		1	
	Interest income		1	
	Gains		2	
	Property business income		1	
	Losses – s.393A current		1	
	– s.393A c/b		2	
	Gift aid		½	
	Unrelieved gift aid		½	9
(b)	*y/e 31.12.05*			
	TWDV b/f		½	
	Additions – no FYA		1	
	Disposals		1	
	Balancing allowance		½	
	WDA		2	
	FYA @ 40%		1	
	FYA @ 100%		1	
	p/e 31.3.06			
	Disposal		½	
	Balancing charge		½	
	WDA – restricted		2	
	FYA @ 40%		1	11
				20

What the examiner said

'This was a two-part question, which involved terminal loss relief for a company and the calculation of capital allowances. The terminal loss relief required a very basic columnar format and easy marks could be earned by 'copying' the figures from the question into the standard layout. The more technical marks were awarded for use of the capital loss – against other capital gains only – and the correct use of the trading loss. The trading loss of the final 12 months of trading can be relieved in the current year, and the previous three years, against any income before gift aid donations. The important point to note here was that the claim period goes back exactly three years prior to the start of the final loss-making period which required the claim in the year ended 30 June 2002 be restricted to six months of the income.

The answers to the capital allowance question were surprisingly poor. This is another area where many marks can be achieved by learning a standard format. A columnar format is always required here with separate columns for plant and machinery, each expensive car and each short-life asset. Entries then follow in the following order – purchases with no first year allowance (FYA), disposals, writing down allowance (WDA) at 25% per annum or a balancing allowance/charge and finally purchases with first year allowance. This procedure should score easy marks. The more technical areas of this question were to appreciate that a 15-month period required two separate calculations with one of 12 months and the other of three. FYA is not apportioned for periods of less than 12 months but WDA is apportioned accordingly. Generally the marks for this question were low and candidates are strongly advised to learn standard layouts in readiness for future sittings.'

42 THE COLLINS BROTHERS

(a) Peter Collins started a road side café business on 1 June 2001. He made up his first set of accounts for the 15 month period ending 31 August 2002 thereafter he made up accounts annually to 31 August, until, due to a lack of custom he was forced to cease business on 31 January 2006. His profits and capital allowances (CAs) for all the periods concerned were as follows.

	Profits	CAs
	£	£
15 months to 31 August 2002	14,000	2,575
12 months to 31 August 2003	15,550	1,550
12 months to 31 August 2004	9,000	1,000
12 months to 31 August 2005	7,400	600
5 months to 31 January 2006	4,200	505

Required

Calculate the FINAL assessment for ALL the years concerned.   (9 marks)

(b) Peter's brother John also started trading on 1 June 2001 but he traded as a company, Collins' Ltd. He made exactly the same trading profits and claimed exactly the same CAs in identical accounting periods and ceased trading on the same day.

Assume that the CAs given for the period ending 31 August 2002 were calculated as £1,925 for the first 12 months and £650 for the remaining period.

The company had no other income or any relevant payments.

Required

Calculate the profits chargeable to corporation tax (PCTCT) for ALL relevant periods of account using the profits of the accounting periods from 1 June 2001 to 31 January 2006.   (6 marks)

(c) *Required*

List five differences in the way in which a person trading as a sole trader is treated for tax and National Insurance purposes compared to operating through a company.   (5 marks)

(20 marks)

42   ANSWER: THE COLLINS BROTHERS

(a)   **Assessments on Peter Collins**

Tax year	Basis period and taxable profits		£
2001/02	Actual basis 1.6.01 – 5.4.02		
	£(14,000 – 2,575) = 11,425 × 10/15		7,617
2002/03	12 months to 31.8.02		
	£11,425 × 12/15		9,140
	(Overlap profits 1.9.01 – 5.4.02		
	£11,425 × 7/15 = £5,332)		
2003/04	Y/e 31.8.03		
	£(15,550 – 1,550)		14,000
2004/05	Y/e 31.8.04		
	£(9,000 – 1,000)		8,000
2005/06	Cessation 1.9.04 – 31.1.06		
	£(7,400 + 4,200 – 600 – 505) =	10,495	5,163
	less overlap profits	(5,332)	

(b)   **Assessments on Collin's Ltd**

A/c period	Taxable profits		£
1.6.01 – 31.5.02	£14,000 × 12/15 =	11,200	
	Less: CAs	(1,925)	9,275
1.6.02 – 31.8.02	£14,000 × 3/15 =	2,800	
	Less: CAs	(650)	2,150
1.9.02 – 31.8.03	£(15,550 – 1,550)		14,000
1.9.03 – 31.8.04	£(9,000 – 1,000)		8,000
1.9.04 – 31.8.05	£(7,400 – 600)		6,800
1.9.05 – 31.1.06	£(4,200 – 505)		3,695

(c)   **Five differences between sole trader/company**

Difference	Sole trader	Company
Tax on profits/gains	Income tax/capital gains tax	Corporation tax on both
Due date for tax on profits	31 January following end of tax year; payments on account may be required	9 months after end of accounting period; no payments on a/c for small/medium company.
Extraction of profits	No further implications	Dividends – savings income Salary – employment income
National insurance	Classes 2 and 4 payable by individual	None on company itself. If salary paid, company pays employer's contributions and individual has employee's contributions deducted.
Use of business assets privately	No further charge; may restrict capital allowances	Charge to income tax may arise as taxable benefits. No restrictions on company's CAs for private use.

Marking guide

			Marks
(a)	2001/02		2
	2002/03		2
	2003/04		1
	2004/05		1
	2005/06	3	9
(b)	1.6.01 – 31.5.02		1
	1.6.02 – 31.8.02		1
	1.9.02 – 31.8.03		1
	1.9.03 – 31.8.04		1
	1.9.04 – 31.8.05		1
	1.9.05 – 31.1.06	1	6
(c)	1 mark for each difference		5
			20

What the examiner said

'The question asked for the differences in the treatment of profits for a company and a sole trader. Many gave exactly the same answer for parts (a) and (b).

For sole traders you are required to quote the relevant tax years for each of the profits – especially important for the opening and closing of a business. For a company there is no such thing as a tax year and you must not quote tax years in your answer. Companies work on an accounting period usually of 12 months. Any period longer than this must be treated as two separate periods one of the first 12 months and the second as the balance.

The theory part of this question was also answered poorly. Many candidates simply had no idea there was a difference. The few good answers quoted aspects such as different rates of tax, different rates of NIC, different payment regimes and benefits.'

43   ALPHABETIC LTD

(a) Alphabetic Ltd makes up annual accounts to 30 September. It paid four quarterly instalments of corporation tax of £156,000 each in respect of the accounting period to 30 September 2005. These were paid on 14 April 2005, 14 July 2005, 14 October 2005 and 14 January 2006. It subsequently transpired that the actual liability for the period was £800,000 and the balance of £176,000 was subsequently paid on 1 July 2006.

Alphabetic Ltd has always paid corporation tax at the full rate.

Required

State the amounts on which interest will be charged in respect of the above accounting period and the dates from which it will run.

(4 marks)

(b) You are required to state what action a company should take if it does not receive a corporation tax return and the penalty for not taking such action.

(2 marks)

(c) You are required to state:

   (i)   the fixed rate penalties for failing to submit a corporation tax return on time; and

(4 marks)

   (ii)   the tax-geared penalties for failing to submit a corporation tax return on time.

(3 marks)

Your answers to (c)(i) and (c)(ii) should indicate under what circumstances these penalties are triggered.

(d) Large companies must normally pay their corporation tax liability by instalments. State the circumstances in which such a company does not need to make instalment payments.

(2 marks)

(15 marks)

Helping hand

Make sure that you know this topic thoroughly before the exam. Straightforward bookwork and revision will lead to a high score on a question like this.

---

43   ANSWER: ALPHABETIC LTD

> **Helping hand**
>
> There are automatic tax geared penalties as well as fixed penalties if a CT return is more than six months late.

(a) Alphabetic Ltd is a 'large' company and as such should have paid its corporation tax liability for the year to 30 September 2005 in four quarterly instalments. The underpayments were:

Due date	*Amount Due*	*Underpaid*
	£	£
14.4.05	200,000	44,000
14.7.05	200,000	44,000
14.10.05	200,000	44,000
14.1.06	200,000	44,000

Interest will run on each of the amounts of £44,000 underpaid from the due date until the date of payment, 1 July 2006.

(b) **If a company has not received a return it must notify HMRC of its liability to corporation tax with 12 months of the end of its accounting period.**

The maximum penalty for not taking such action is 100% of the corporation tax unpaid twelve months after the end of the accounting period.

(c) (i)   **Fixed rate penalties**

(1) **Where the return is up to 3 months late - £100**

(2) **Where the return is more than 3 months late - £200**

(3) **Where the return is the third consecutive one to be filed late the above penalties are increased to £500 and £1,000 respectively.**

(ii)   **A tax geared penalty is triggered in addition to the fixed penalties if a return is more than six months late. The penalty is 10% of any tax unpaid six months after the return was due if the total delay is up to 12 months, but 20% of that tax if the return is over 12 months late.**

(d) **Companies that become large during an accounting period will not have to pay their corporation tax for that period by instalments if:**

(i)   **their taxable profits for the period do not exceed £10 million** (reduced if there are associated companies); **and**

(ii)   **they were not a large company in the previous period**

A 'large company' is one that pays corporation tax at the full rate.

Also, there is a de minimis limit in that any company whose liability does not exceed £10,000 need not pay by instalments.

44   NAC PLC

(a) NAC plc is a UK resident company and has the following results for its 10 month accounting period ending 31 December 2005:

	£	£
Trading profit after charging the following:		476,000
Depreciation	20,000	
Entertainment of customers	5,000	
Debenture interest (note 1)	4,000	
Legal fees (note 2)	3,500	

In addition the company received:

	£	
Rent	20,000	(amount due)
UK dividend	9,000	(cash received)

A capital gain of £16,000 was made on 14 October 2005.

A Gift Aid donation amounting to £7,000 was paid on 15 November 2005.

The following amounts were brought forward as at 1 March 2005.

Capital loss	£5,000
Trading loss	£80,000

Note 1. The interest was the amount paid on 14 July in respect of debentures issued to purchase a machine used in the business. An amount of £2,000 (gross) was still owed for the 10 month period ending 31 December 2005. All the debentureholders were individuals.

Note 2. The legal fees consisted of:

Fees for debt collecting	£500
Fees for renewing a long lease	£1,500
Fees for issuing debentures	£1,500

Note 3. The company has made no claim for capital allowances for the period to 31 December 2005.

Required

Calculate the total corporation tax liability of NAC plc for the period ending 31 December 2005.   (16 marks)

(b) A large UK resident company has Profits Chargeable to Corporation Tax (PCTCT) of £1,800,000 for its 12 month accounting period ending 31 March 2006.

Required

Calculate the amount of corporation tax payable and state the dates on which payments must be made.   (4 marks)

(20 marks)

44 ANSWER: NAC PLC

(a) **NAC plc Corporation Tax payable for 10 month accounting period to 31.12.05**

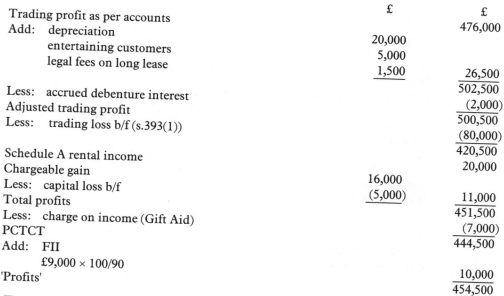

		£	£
Trading profit as per accounts			476,000
Add: depreciation		20,000	
entertaining customers		5,000	
legal fees on long lease		1,500	26,500
			502,500
Less: accrued debenture interest			(2,000)
Adjusted trading profit			500,500
Less: trading loss b/f (s.393(1))			(80,000)
			420,500
Schedule A rental income			20,000
Chargeable gain		16,000	
Less: capital loss b/f		(5,000)	11,000
Total profits			451,500
Less: charge on income (Gift Aid)			(7,000)
PCTCT			444,500
Add: FII			
£9,000 × 100/90			10,000
'Profits'			454,500

Tax liability

As this is a 10 month period, the limits for SCR must be scaled down:

			FY04 and FY05
Upper limit	£1,500,000 × 10/12		£1,250,000
Lower limit	£300,000 × 10/12		£250,000

Small companies' marginal relief applies in both financial years

FY04

	£
1/10 × £444,500 × 30%	13,335
Less: Small companies' marginal relief	
$£(1,250,000 - 454,500) \times \dfrac{444,500}{454,500} \times \dfrac{11}{400} \times 1/10$	(2,139)

FY05

	£
£444,500 × 30% × 9/10	120,015
Less: $(£1,250,000 - 454,500) \times \dfrac{444,500}{454,500} \times 11/400 \times 9/10$	(19,256)
Corporation tax payable	111,955

Note. As the corporation tax rates and limits did not change, there is strictly no need to split the above into financial years when calculating the corporation tax.

(b) Corporation tax payable

£1,800,000 × 30%	£540,000

As the company is a large company, this amount is payable by instalments

Payable in four equal instalments of	£135,000

Due on:

14 October 2005
14 January 2006
14 April 2006
14 July 2006

Marking guide

		Marks	
(a)	Profits per a/cs	$^1/_2$	
	Customers' entertainment	$^1/_2$	
	Long lease fees	1	
	Accrued debenture interest	2	
	Trading profit		1
	Loss relief	1	
	Property business income	$^1/_2$	
	Gain	$^1/_2$	
	Capital loss	1	
	Gift aid	1	
	FII	1	
	SCR limits	1	
	Tax @ 30%	2	
	Marginal relief	3	
			16
(b)	CT payable	1	
	Instalment amounts	1	
	Dates for instalments	2	
			4
			20

What the examiner said

'A two part question requiring a standard corporation tax assessment and a calculation of payments under the quarterly payment system for large companies. Part (a) was generally well attempted but many candidates missed the point of the 10 month period. The quarterly payment system for large companies was a mystery to most overseas candidates.'

45   **QUESTION WITH HELP: DAVID**

David has been trading successfully as a carpenter for many years. He is registered for VAT, and has quarterly accounting periods based on calendar quarters. He has produced the following statement for his business for the 12 months to 31 December 2005 (all figures exclude VAT):

	£	£
Services performed (Note 1)		68,000
Less expenses:		
Bank overdraft interest	280	
New tools (bought July 2005)	2,000	
Telephone (Note 2)	440	
Motor expenses (Note 3)	17,960	
Profit		(20,680)
		47,320

Notes:

(1)   During the year to 31 December 2005, David's work has been invoiced as follows:

	£
February	14,000
March	4,000
June	10,000
September	6,000
October	22,000
December	12,000
	68,000

(2)   The telephone bills were due and paid in equal amounts each quarter.

(3)   Motor expenses (all from VAT registered suppliers) comprise the following:

	£
Fuel (£80 per month and no private mileage)	960
Servicing (March 2005)	200
Repairs (April 2005)	800
New car (invoiced 1 December 2005)	16,000
	17,960

Required

Calculate the VAT payable for each VAT accounting period, and state the due date for payment of the tax. The car had an element of private use.

> If you are stuck, look at the next page for detailed help as to how you should tackle this question.

APPROACHING THE ANSWER

Step 1	Work out the VAT quarters
Step 2	Allocate the invoices to each quarter
Step 3	Work out the output tax for each quarter
Step 4	Allocate the expenses to each quarter. Is there any irrecoverable tax?
Step 5	Work out the input tax for each quarter
Step 6	Deduct input tax from output tax for each quarter
Step 7	Don't forget to state the due date for payment of the VAT due

45 **ANSWER TO QUESTION WITH HELP: DAVID**

	Quarter ended			
	31.3.05	*30.6.05*	*30.9.05*	*31.12.05*
	£	£	£	£
Outputs				
Invoice work	18,000	10,000	6,000	34,000
Output VAT 17.5%	3,150	1,750	1,050	5,950
Inputs				
Telephone	110	110	110	110
New tools			2,000	
Fuel	240	240	240	240
Servicing	200			
Repairs		800		
	550	1,150	2,350	350
Input VAT thereon	96.25	201.25	411.25	61.25
Net VAT payable	3,053.75	1,548.75	638.75	5,888.75
Due date	30.4.05	31.7.05	31.10.05	31.1.06

VAT on the new car is not recoverable as it is used privately.

46   PETER

On 2 October 2005 Peter, a qualified plumber, issued an invoice to Bigbuilders Limited. The invoice was due for payment by 10 October 2005. The company writes back on 15 October 2005 stating that although they are not disputing the invoice they do not feel they can afford to pay. On 31 January 2006 Peter has still not been paid and therefore decides to write off the debt in his books and records.

Required

(a) Assuming Peter makes a VAT return to 30 November 2005 and quarterly thereafter, state which return is the earliest return in which he can claim VAT bad debt relief.

(2 marks)

(b) State the conditions which Peter must satisfy for a claim to be made.   (5 marks)

(7 marks)

46   ANSWER: PETER

(a) The debt is **six months** old on 10 April 2006.

The return in which bad debt relief can therefore be claimed is thus the return for the quarter ended 30 May 2006.

(b) To be entitled to make a claim for bad debt relief, Peter must satisfy the below conditions:

(i)   **VAT due on the supply must have been accounted for;**

(ii) The **amount outstanding must have been written off** in his accounts as a bad debt;

(iii) **Six months must have passed from when payment became due;**

(iv) The **claim for bad debt relief must be made within three years;**

(v)   Peter must have a **copy of the VAT invoice and records** to show that the VAT has been accounted for and the debt written off.

Marking guide

		Marks	
(a)	Debt at least 6 months old	1	
	¼ in which falls	1	2
(b)	One mark for each point		5
			7

BPP
PROFESSIONAL EDUCATION

47   **CAVE**

For the year ended 31 March 2006 Mr Cave had the following (VAT exclusive) transactions:

	£
Sales at standard rate (17.5%)	1,700,000
Sales at zero rate	400,000
Plant sold in UK	100,000
Plant sold to overseas customer (not EU)	50,000
Purchases at standard rate (17.5%)	600,000
Purchases at zero rate	100,000
Wages	900,000
Motor car (purchased new, 50% business use)	5,000

The above amounts do not include any VAT.

No private fuel of the car is paid for by the business.

The plant was sold for less than its original cost to the business.

Required

(a) Calculate the amount of output tax which he would be required to account for and how much input tax could be deducted therefrom for the year ended 31 March 2006.
(6 marks)

(b) Calculate the capital allowances which could be claimed by him for the year ended 31 March 2006 assuming a general pool of £92,290 at 1 April 2005.
(6 marks)

(**12 marks**)

Helping hand

What is the VAT status of supplies to overseas customers?

---

47   **ANSWER: CAVE**

Helping hand

Supplies to overseas customers are zero rated.

(a)

		£	VAT £
Output Tax			
Outputs at standard rate £ (1,700,000 + 100,000 plant)		1,800,000	315,000
Outputs at zero rate £ (400,000 + 50,000 overseas plant)		450,000	
Total taxable outputs		2,250,000	
Input tax			
Inputs chargeable at 17.5%		600,000	(105,000)
			210,000

(b) Capital allowances for the year ending 31 March 2006

	Car (50% private use) £	Pool £	Allowances £
TWDV 1.4.05			
Additions: motor car			
(£5,000 plus £875 VAT)	5,875	92,290	
Disposals: (plant)		(150,000)	
		(57,710)	(57,710) BC
WDA × 25%	(1,469) × 50%		735
TWDV 31.3.06	4,406		(56,975) BC

Marking guide

			Marks	
(a)	Standard rate outputs		1	
	Output VAT		1	
	Zero rate outputs		1	
	Inputs chargeable at Standard rate		1	
	Input VAT		1	
	Net VAT payable		1	6
(b)	TWDV b/f		½	
	Addition		½	
	Disposal		2	
	BC		½	
	WDA		1	
	Total allowances (net)		1	6
				12

48 LEGG LTD

Legg Ltd is registered for VAT. In the quarter ended 30 September 2005, it had the following transactions:

	£
Purchases	
Stock for resale	130,000
Office furniture	2,000
Fuel for cars	1,800
Business entertaining	350
Sales	
Stock	250,000

All amounts are VAT inclusive.

The fuel for cars includes private fuel for one car (1,600cc) provided to an employee. The VAT inclusive fuel scale charge for this car is £311 per quarter.

Required

Calculate the VAT payable by Legg Ltd for the quarter. **(8 marks)**

48   ANSWER: LEGG LTD

	£	£
Output VAT		
Stock sold £250,000 × $^7/_{47}$		37,234
Private fuel £311 × $^7/_{47}$		46
		37,280
Input VAT		
Stock purchased £130,000 × $^7/_{47}$	19,362	
Office furniture £2,000 × $^7/_{47}$	298	
Business entertaining – irrecoverable	nil	
Petrol £1,800 × $^7/_{47}$	268	(19,928)
VAT payable		17,352

Marking guide

	Marks
Output VAT	
Stock	1
Fuel	2
Input VAT	
Stock	1
Office furniture	1
Business entertaining – irrecoverable	1
Petrol	1
VAT payable	1
	8

BPP
PROFESSIONAL EDUCATION

49   CITY MERCHANDISE (06/04)

City Merchandise Ltd prepares value added tax (VAT) returns on a quarterly basis. It does not operate the cash accounting scheme. During the company's quarter ended 31 March 2006 the following transactions occurred:

	£
Standard rated sales	110,000
Zero-rated sales	30,000
Standard rated purchases	60,000

The above three amounts are stated exclusive of VAT where applicable.

The company offers a 5% discount to customers who pay within 30 days. This discount is offered on all sales but only 50% of customers settle within the discount period.

The company also paid the following expenses during the same VAT quarter:

	£
Electricity	4,000
Wages	28,000
Accountancy fees	1,000
Machine repairs	2,500

The above four amounts are stated inclusive of VAT where applicable.

Required

Calculate the VAT due for the quarter ended 31 March 2006 and state by when this amount must be paid.   **(6 marks)**

49   ANSWER: CITY MERCHANDISE

VAT due year end 31.3.06

	£	£
Standard rated sales £110,000 × 17.5% × 95% (N1)		18,287
Less:		
Standard rated purchases		
£60,000 × 17.5%	10,500	
Electricity		
£4,000 × $\frac{7}{47}$	596	
Accounting		
£1,000 × $\frac{7}{47}$	149	
Machine repairs		
£2,500 × $\frac{7}{47}$	372	(11,617)
VAT due 30.4.06		6,670

Notes: 1.   Where discount offered for prompt payment, VAT is charged on the net amount whether or not the discount is taken up.

2.   Wages outside scope of VAT.

Marking guide

	Marks
Standard rate sales	2
Standard rate purchases	½
Electricity ½	
Accounting ½	
Repairs ½	
Due date 1	
Wages outside scope	1
	6

What the examiner said

This question required a calculation of VAT for a quarterly return. This is new to the syllabus and candidates should have been expecting this. Some obviously were and showed very good understanding but many had obviously overlooked this area and little if any studying had been done on this. The main problems were: for exclusive figures a percentage of 17.5% should because to calculate the tax whereas a fraction of 7/47 should be used for inclusive figures; when calculating VAT discounts should be taken in full even when not taken by the customer; wages are outside the scope of VAT and should therefore be ignored and finally the payment of VAT is due 30 days after the quarter end ie 30 April 2006 in this case.

50   **ACCOUNTSRUS (12/04)**

You are a tax technician working for AccountsRUs, a small accountancy firm. Your line manager has asked you to reply to a letter, received on 6 December 2006 from a new client.

The letter is from John Starr, the managing director of Help4U Ltd, a newly formed company situated in Leeds. He has asked for advice on the value added tax (VAT) registration rules.

Required:

Draft a letter to John Starr giving brief details of the compulsory registration rules for VAT.

Your letter should include:

-    details of when compulsory registration for VAT is due
-    the dates by which HMRC must be notified of registration; and
-    the effective date of registration.

(Details of voluntary registration for VAT and the rules on deregistration from VAT are not required.)

Marks will be awarded for the style and presentation of your answer.   **(8 marks)**

50   ANSWER: ACCOUNTSRUS

AccountsRUs
1 Borough Street
Leeds LE1

John Starr
Help4U Ltd
22 The Street
Anywhere
England

10 December 2006

Dear John

VAT REGISTRATION

In response to your letter of 6 December 2006, I have detailed below the compulsory registration rules for VAT.

Compulsory registration

Compulsory registration is required if one of the following two tests is met.

(1)   *Historic test*

At the end of any month, the cumulative turnover (excluding VAT) of taxable supplies in the previous 12 months exceeded £60,000.

(2)   *Future test*

If at any time it is forecast that turnover (excluding VAT) of taxable supplies in the next 30 days will exceed £60,000.

Notification

In both cases, HM Revenue and Customs (HMRC) must be notified within 30 days. For the *historic test* notification is due within 30 days of the month end. For the *future test*, the deadline for HMRC to receive notification of registration coincides with the end of the 30 day period.

Effective date

Registration will be effective from the end of the month following the month in which the £60,000 was exceeded for the *historic test*. For the *future test*, registration is effective from the start of the 30 day period.

I hope this has answered your queries but in the meantime if you have any further queries please do not hesitate to contact me.

Yours sincerely

A N Other

Marking guide	Marks
Presentation	2
12 month historic test	1
30 day future test	1
Notification to HMCE	2
Effective registration date	2
	8

What the examiner said

'This question required candidates to write a letter to a client explaining the VAT registration rules. Two marks were available for the style and presentation of the letter and indeed many candidates scored these two marks and none for the content! The requirement was clear in what information to given in the letter but many decided to 'waffle' on just about everything they knew about VAT rather than sticking to the requirement, few marks if any were awarded for this approach. Candidates must stick to the requirement given and not invent their own.'

Mock Exams

Preparing taxation computations
June 2005

Question Paper	
Time allowed	3 hours
ALL FOUR questions are compulsory and MUST be attempted	

Advanced Level
Paper 9

ALL four questions are compulsory and MUST be attempted.

1   **RAVI PATEL**

(a)   Ravi Patel is a computer expert working for a UK resident company receiving an annual salary of £39,000.

    During the tax year 2005/06 Ravi received the following benefits.

    (i)   The use of a company owned apartment. This had cost the company £160,000 in May 2004 and has been occupied by Ravi since that date. The apartment has an annual rateable value of £4,100 and Ravi pays the company £2,500 a year for its use. The occupation of the apartment is not regarded as job-related.

    (ii)   Furniture valued at £12,000 is provided for use in the apartment. During 2005/06 the company paid decorating bills of £550 and wages to a cleaner amounting to £1,500.

    (iii)   A 2.0 litre diesel BMW car, with CO_2 emission rate of 204g per km and a recommended list of price of £26,500. This was first provided for Ravi's use in July 2004. Accessories amounting to £800 were added when the car was first provided. Ravi contributed £4,000 towards the capital cost of the car. The car is used 20% for business use and 80% for private use. The company pays for all the fuel but Ravi contributes £40 per month towards this cost.

    In addition to the above the company also paid £750 to the local golf club in respect of Ravi's 2005/06 membership and refunded £1,325 to Ravi in respect of actual business expenses incurred whilst he was away on official trips.

    Ravi had agreed with the company that it would deduct £20 a month during the whole of 2005/06 in respect of charitable payments under the payroll deduction scheme.

    Ravi paid £234 (net) per month to a private pension plan. In February 2006 he paid an additional lump sum of £2,340 (net) to the same plan. In December 2005 he paid £180 fees to an HMRC approved professional body related to his employment.

    Ravi paid tax of £7,808 under the PAYE system for 2005/06.

    In addition to the above Ravi received the following income during 2005/06.

    (i)   Bank interest of £240

    (ii)   Building society interest of £190

    (iii)   Dividends from shares held in UK companies amounting to £280

    (iv)   Dividends from investments held in Individual Savings Account (ISA) amounting to £145

    The above amounts are all stated at the cash amounts received.

    Required:

    Calculate the income tax payable by Ravi for the tax year 2005/06   (23 marks)

(b)   Ravi's wife, Neta, started her own business on 1 October 2003. Her first sets of adjusted profits after capital allowances were:

	£
Period to 30 April 2004	8,680
Year to 30 April 2005	18,720
Year to April 2006	22,080

    Required:

    (i)   **Calculate Neta's trading profits for her first three years of assessment. You are not required to calculate any overlap profit.**   (5 marks)

    (ii)   **Calculate Neta's total national insurance contributions for 2005/06.**   (3 marks)

    (iii)   **State when income tax for 2005/06 will be paid and how payment will be calculated. You are not required to calculate the actual amount of each payment.**   (3 marks)

    (34 marks)

2   **THOMPSON BROTHERS LTD**

(a)   Thompson Brothers Ltd is a UK resident company with no associated companies. Up to 2005 the company had always made up its accounts to 31 March annually but because of new accounting policies the company decided to change its accounting date to 31 December.

The adjusted trading profit before capital allowances for the 9-month period ended 31 December 2005 was £256,663.

Other income and expenditure received and paid in the same period was:

Income

	£
Dividends from UK companies	18,000
Rental income (note 1)	10,000
Debenture interest (note 2)	3,000
Capital profit (note 3)	36,000

Expenditure

	£
Interest for late payment of tax	2,000
Gift aid payment to a UK registered charity	7,000

Notes

1   The rent was received in two equal amounts on 1 April 2005 and 1 October 2005 and was in each case in respect of the following six months.

2   Debenture interest is received six monthly on 31 March and 30 September each year and is in respect of a holding of £120,000 5% Loan Stock.

3   The profit shown is in respect of an unused office block purchased for £60,000 in December 2004 and sold for £86,000 in October 2005. (Indexation factor December 2004 – October 2005: 0.028.)

A capital loss of £4,000 was brought forward as at 1 April 2005.

The company purchased a new factory in September 2005 for £150,000, which included £30,000 for land. The company has not claimed rollover relief.

The tax written down value on the company's plant and machinery pool as at 1 April 2005 was £140,000. During the period ended 31 December 2005 the company purchased plant for £80,000 and a new car (which is not a low emission car) for one of the director's private use at a cost of £22,000. An old machine, which had originally cost £28,000, was sold for £23,000 in November 2005.

The company is classified as medium sized for capital allowances purposes.

Required:

(i)   **Calculate Thompson Brothers Ltd's total capital allowances for both plant and machinery and industrial buildings for the nine-month period ended 31 December 2005.**   (7 marks)

(ii)   **Calculate the corporation tax payable by Thompson Brothers Ltd for the nine-month period ended 31 December 2005.**   (11 marks)

(b)   Parker plc is a large resident UK company. In its accounting year ended 31 March 2006 it had estimated its profits chargeable to corporation tax (PCTCT) to be £1,600,000. The company had PCTCT amounting to £1,800,000 in the year to 31 March 2005.

Required:

In respect of the chargeable accounting period ended 31 March 2006.

(i)   **Calculate the corporation tax payable.**   (1 mark)

(ii)   **State the due dates of payment of the tax and the amount of each of those payments.**

(4 marks)

(23 marks)

3   **FIONA BANKS**

(a) Fiona Banks is a UK resident and had the following transactions in capital items during 2005/06.

14 June 2005. Sold a factory for £228,000. This had originally been purchased in May 1994 for £120,000 and had been enlarged at a cost of £35,000 in August 2002. The indexed cost of the factory on 6 April 1998 was £138,240. The factory had always been used as a business asset.

11 November 2005. Sold a painting for £9,870. Auctioneer's fees of 10% were payable on this amount. The painting had been purchased in June 1999 for £2,500. It has never been used as a business asset.

Fiona had unused capital losses brought forward on 6 April 2005 amounting to £3,400.

Fiona's statutory total income (STI) for 2005/06 was £34,720.

Required:

Calculate the capital gains tax payable by Fiona for the tax year 2005/06.   (10 marks)

(b) Jane Bush purchased a non-business asset in September 2000 for £18,000. It was destroyed by a flash flood in November 2005. Jane replaced the asset in March 2006 at a cost of £28,000 having received £29,500 compensation from an insurance company.

Required:

(i)   **Calculate the chargeable gain arising in 2005/06.**   (3 marks)

(ii)   **State the base cost of the replacement asset.**   (1 mark)

(c) Peter Stone purchased his main residence on 1 July 1985 for £54,500. He moved into the property immediately and occupied it until he moved abroad to take up employment on 1 September 1987. He retuned to the UK and reoccupied the property on 1 May 1992. He remained in the property until 1 January 1993 when he moved to another UK city on a temporary work secondment. On 1 January 1998 he returned to the property. On 1 March 2000 he moved to his parents home to take care of his sick mother. The property was finally sold on 1 July 2005. Peter never returned to the property after 1 March 2000.

Required:

Using a tabular format state, giving reasons in each case, the deemed and actual periods of occupation and the periods of non-occupation of the property.   (8 marks)

(22 marks)

4   **SUSAN CHANCE**

(a) Susan Chance runs a small business from home which she commenced in 1997. Her recent adjusted trading results (after capital allowances) have been:

	£
Year ended 31 December 2003	12,500
Year ended 31 December 2004	(15,000) loss
Year ended 31 December 2005	3,400

Susan has other income of £8,000 in 2003/04, £4,000 in 2004/05 and £26,000 in 2005/06.

She has written to you asking for advice on the use of the 2004 trading loss.

Required:

Write a letter to Susan, using any fictitious addresses, advising her on the use of the loss. Your letter should provide details of :

(i)   **the years in which the loss can be used;**
(ii)   **the income it can be used against; and**
(iii) **three planning points to consider when deciding which claim to make**

(Note you are not required to make a final decision or to show any calculations).   (8 marks)
                                                        Presentation (2 marks)

(b) Monty Finch has been trading for the last three years. His annual sales have recently exceeded the VAT threshold of £60,000 but he has failed to notify HMRC.

Required:

State the amount(s) of late notification penalty that could be applied.   (5 marks)

(c) Bob Hawkes operates a jewellery business and is registered for VAT. He received an order for a silver and diamond necklace on 14 May 2005. A deposit of £350 was received with the order. The order was completed and delivered on 16 July 2005. An invoice was raised and despatched on 20 July 2005 and the final (balancing) payment was received on 31 August 2005.

Bob does not operate the cash accounting scheme.

Required:

State how the tax point for VAT purposes is determined and the date(s) which will apply in this case.
(6 marks)

(21 marks)

MOCK EXAM 1
ANSWERS

DO NOT TURN THIS PAGE UNTIL YOU
HAVE COMPLETED MOCK EXAM 1

WARNING! APPLYING THE MARKING SCHEME

If you decide to mark your paper using the marking scheme (reproduced at the end of each BPP suggested solution), you should bear in mind the following points.

1   The BPP solutions are not definitive: you will see that we have applied our own interpretation of the marking scheme to our solutions to show how good answers should gain marks, but there may be more than one way to answer the question. You must try to judge fairly whether different points made in your answers are correct and relevant and therefore worth marks according to the marking scheme.

2   In numerical answers, do not penalise yourself too much for minor arithmetical errors: if you have followed the correct principles you should gain most of the marks. This emphasises the importance of including workings, which show the marker which principles you were following.

3   If you have a friend or colleague who is studying or has studied this paper, you might ask him or her to mark your paper for you, thus gaining a more objective assessment. Remember you and your friend are not trained or objective markers, so try to avoid complacency or pessimism if you appear to have done very well or very badly.

1   RAVI PATEL

> **Tutorial note.** Remember the question does not have to be answered in the order presented. The examiner often puts a stand-alone knowledge based requirements that are quick to answer towards the end of the question.
>
> If the question gives you a monthly amount, like £234 private pension contribution, £20 charity donation, it must be multiplied by 12 to give the annual amount to be included in the computation.
>
> Don't confuse charity donations under the payroll deduction scheme (ie Give As You Earn) that are deducted from gross salary, with gift aid donations, that extend the basis rate band.

(a)   **Ravi Patel income tax 2005/06**

	Non-savings	Savings (excl dividend)	Dividend	Total
	£	£	£	£
Salary	39,000			
Accommodation (W1)	5,850			
Furniture (W2)	2,400			
Decoration bill	550			
Cleaner's wages	1,500			
Car (W3)	6,990			
Fuel (W4)	4,320			
Golf membership	750			
Business expenses	nil			
Less: Give As You Earn (£20 × 12)	(240)			
Less: professional fees	(180)			
Bank interest £240 × $\frac{100}{80}$		300		
BSI £190 × $\frac{100}{80}$		237		
Dividends £280 × $\frac{100}{90}$			311	
STI	60,940	537	311	61,788
Less: PA	(4,895)		311	(4,895)
	56,045	537	311	56,893

Note. Business expenses not taxable because incurred wholly exclusively and necessarily for employment.

Workings

1   **Accommodation (not job related)**

	£
Annual value	4,100
Add: additional charge (£160,000 – £75,000) × 5%	4,250
Less: employee contribution	(2,500)
	5,850

2   **Furniture**

£12,000 × 20% = £2,400

3   **Car**

$$\frac{200-140}{5} = 12 + 15 + 3 \text{ (diesel)} = 30\%$$

£(26,500 + 800 - 4,000) = £23,300 × 30% = £6,990

Note. No apportionment for business and private use.

4   **Fuel**

   £14,400 × 30% = £4,320

   Note. No reduction for employee contribution towards private use fuel.

5   **Private pension**

   $(234 \times 12) = 2,808 + £2,340 = £5,184 \times \dfrac{100}{78} = £6,600$

Tax

	£	£
Non-savings income		
£2,090 × 10%		209
£(32,400 – 2,090) = 30,310 × 22%		6,668
£6,600 (W5) × 22% (private pension)		1,452
£(56,045 – 32,400 – 6,600) = 17,045 × 40%		6,818
Savings income		
£537 × 40%		215
Dividend income		
£311 × 32.5%		101
		15,463
Less: PAYE	7,808	
Savings £537 × 20%	107	
Dividends £311 × 10%	31	
		(7,946)
Tax payable		7,517

(b) (i)   **Trading profits for 2003/04 to 2005/06**

Fiscal year		£	*Trading profit* £
2003/04	1st year – Actual 1.10.03 – 5.4.04 6/7 × £8,680		7,440
2004/05	2nd year – 1st 12 months 1.10.03 – 30.4.04 1.5.04 – 30.9.04 5/12 × £18,720	8,680 7,800	16,480
2005/06	3rd year – period of account ending in tax year y/e 30.4.05		18,720

(ii)   **Sole Trader's National Insurance Contributions**

		£
Class 2	£2.10 × 52 weeks =	109
Class 4	£(18,720 – 4,895) × 8% =	1,106
		1,215

(iii)   **Income tax payment dates for 2005/06**

   Payments on account: 31 January 2006 and 31 July 2006:
                          each payment is 50% of the income tax due for 2004/05

   Final payment: 31 January 2007:
                          balance of any income tax due for 2005/06

Marking guide

			Marks
(a) (i)		Salary	½
		Accommodation	2
		Furniture	1
		Wages and bills	1
		Car	4
		Fuel	1
		Golf fees	1
		Reimbursed travel expenses	½
		Give As You Earn	1
		Professional fees	1
		Bank interest	1
		Building society interest	1
		Dividends	1
		Personal allowance	½
		ISA interest is exempt	½
		Tax at 10%, 22%, 40% and 32.5%	2½
		Extended Basic Rate Band	2
		Tax deducted	1½
			23
(b) (i)		1st year – 2003/04	2
		2nd year – 2004/05	2
		3rd year – 2005/06	1
			5
	(ii)	Class 2	1
		Class 4	2
			3
	(iii)	Dates	1½
		Amounts	1½
			3
			34

What the examiner said

This was a two-part question testing the candidates' knowledge of income tax assessments, opening year rules of trading income, National Insurance contributions (NIC) and payment dates for income tax.

Part (a) was very well attempted with most candidates demonstrating sound knowledge of income tax assessments. Layouts were generally very good with nearly all candidates categorising the income correctly into non-savings, savings and dividend with only a few confusing savings and dividends by adding them together.

The most common mistake in this question was for candidates to extend the basic rate band by the charitable payment. Where an individual contributes to a charity under the payroll giving scheme then the annual amount contributed is simply deducted from the individual's employment income before it is taxed – it does not affect the basic rate band. It is donations via the gift aid scheme, which are paid net of 22% tax with the gross amount extending the basic rate band.

The other common mistakes made by candidates included:

- taxing ISA interest – this is tax free
- not grossing up the pension contribution before extending the basic rate band
- taxing savings and dividend income at the wrong rates
- not rounding down the car benefit percentage and not adding 3% for it being diesel
- confusing the capital contribution towards the car and deducting it from the benefit instead of the list price

Part (b) produced a mixed standard of answers, with many giving very good answers to part (i) but poor answers to parts (ii) and (iii).

Part (i) required candidates to calculate the opening year assessments for a sole trader and this in general was answered well by most, however candidates are reminded that in this sort of question they must state the tax years correctly (eg.2003-2004) not simply year 1, year 2 etc.

Part (ii) required the calculation of NIC. Too many candidates confused class 2 and class 4 for a sole trader (which were required here) with class 1 and 1A (which are for employees and their employers).

Part (iii) required knowledge of income tax payment dates for a sole trader. The biggest mistake here was that candidates did not make it clear in their answers how the amount due on each date was calculated, eg. 50% of the last year's total income tax and NIC.'

2 THOMPSON BROTHERS LTD

> **Tutorial note**. For a short accounting period the 25% writing down allowance and the restricted £3,000 for expensive cars have to be time apportioned, but not first year allowances. Remember property business income and income interest are on an accruals basis ie what *should* have been received less what *should* have been paid.
>
> To identify the correct corporation tax rate the 'profits' earned in the 9 month accounting period should not be compared with £1,500,000 and £300,0000 but prorated SCR limits instead.
>
> The 5 marks allocated to part (b) highlights that more than one amount and date are required for the corporation tax payment. Please note, the examiner is not asking you to repeat your answer to question 1 part (b)(iii). Payment dates for corporation tax are not the same as income tax.

(a) (i) **Capital allowances**

Plant and machinery - 9 month period ended 31.12.05

	FYA £	Pool £	Car £	Allowances £
TWDV b/f		140,000		
Addition not qualifying for FYA			22,000	
Disposals (Note)		(23,000)		
		117,000	22,000	
WDA @ 25% × 9/12		(21,938)		21,938
WDA @ £3,000 max × 9/12			(2,250)	2,250
		95,062	19,750	
Addition qualifying for FYA @ 40%	80,000 (32,000)			32,000
		48,000		
TWDV c/f		143,062	19,750	56,188

Note. No time apportioning of FYA for short accounting period

Industrial buildings – 9m period ended 31.12.05

	£
Cost	150,000
Less: land	(30,000)
	120,000

$$£120,000 \times 4\% \times \frac{9}{12} = £3,600$$

Note. IBA time apportioned according to length of short accounting period (ie 9m) not according to purchase date of factory.

Total allowances are therefore:

£(56,188 + 3,600) = £59,788

(ii) **Corporation tax computation – 9m period ended 31.2.05**

	£	£
Adjusted trading profits	256,663	
Less: capital allowances	(59,788)	
Trading income		196,875
Property business income – accruals ($£10,000 \times \dfrac{9}{12}$		7,500

Interest income

	£	£
debenture interest – accruals $£120,000 \times 5\% \times \dfrac{9}{12}$	4,500	
interest for late tax payment	(2,000)	
		2,500
Capital gain (W)		20,320
Less: Charges on income		
Gift aid		(7,000)
PCTCT		220,195
Add: FII $18,000 \times \dfrac{100}{90}$		20,000
'Profits'		240,195

Workings

Capital gain

	£
Proceeds	86,000
Less: cost	(60,000)
	26,000
Less: indexation $£(60,000 \times 0.028)$	(1,680)
Gain	24,320
Less: capital loss b/f	(4,000)
Net capital gain	20,320

SCR limits

Lower	£300,000	9/12	£225,000
Upper	£1,500,000	9/12	£1,125,000

Therefore, full rate less marginal relief applies.

Tax liability

	£
$£220,195 \times 30\%$	66,058
Less: marginal relief	
$\dfrac{11}{400} \times (1125,000 - 240,195)\ \dfrac{220,195}{240,195}$	(22,306)
	43,752

(b) (i) **Parker plc – corporation tax payable**

SCR limits

Upper	£1,500,000
Therefore full rate applies $£1,600,000 \times 30\% =$	£480,000

(ii) As Parker plc is large (ie pays corporation tax at full rate and does not benefit from exemption for first year paying tax at full rate) this amount is payable by four equal quarterly instalments.

Due on:	*Amount*
	£
14 October 2005 (14th of 7th moth)	120,000
14 January 2006	120,000
14 April 2006	120,000
14 July 2006	120,000

Marking guide

			Marks
(a)	(i)	TWDV b/f	½
		Additions	1
		Disposal	½
		WDA	2
		FYA	1
		IBA	2
			7
	(ii)	Trading income	1
		Property business income	1
		Interest income	2
		Capital gain	2½
		Gift aid	½
		FII	1
		Adjusted SCR limits	1
		Corporation tax calculation	2
			11
(b)	(i)	Tax at full rate	1
	(ii)	Due dates	2
		Amounts	2
			4
			23

What the examiner said

'This was a two-part question involving three common areas of corporation tax, capital allowances, a corporation tax assessment and payment dates for a large company.

Part (a) (i) required calculations of capital allowances for both plant and machinery and industrial buildings for a nine-month period. For candidates that had learnt the standard layout of a capital allowances calculation there were some simple marks to be earned, however many had not learnt this layout and as a result presented their answers using various incorrect methods and earned themselves very few marks. The standard layout is demonstrated in both the recommended texts books and the suggested answers to this paper and this should be used in all future answers.

Common errors in this part included:

- not pooling items correctly
- not restricting WDA to nine months
- restricting FYA
- using the incorrect % for FYA
- applying WDA to the full cost of the building without deducting the cost of the land

Part (a) (ii) required a calculation of corporation tax for the same nine-month period. Most candidates were able to make a good attempt at this but several were confused by the adjusted profit given in the question. Where the question refers to a trading profit as being adjusted it means that any income or expenditure that should not form part of the profit for tax purposes has already been deducted from or added back to the accounting profit and therefore the figure given does not need further adjustment for these items. Unfortunately several candidates waste time and effort readjusting the amount given for the other items of income and expenditure given in the question.

Candidates should further note that the basic calculation required:

- property business income to be assessed on the accruals basis (9/12 of the annual amount)
- interest income also to be calculated on the accruals basis with the amount of interest on late payment of tax to be netted off to give one total for interest income
- the capital loss to be deducted from the capital gain – not from the total income
- the dividend received to be grossed up by 100/90 before adding it to PCTCT
- the tax rate thresholds to be reduced to 9/12 before determining the appropriate rate of tax

Part (b) involved calculating the tax for a large company and stating the dates on which this should be paid. Many incorrectly used the amount for the period ending 31 March 2005, which was only given to confirm that the company had previously been large and therefore the quarterly payment system was to be used for the period ending 31 March 2006.

Many candidates scored well here but many also had no idea that tax for a large company is normally paid in four instalments on the 14th day of the 7th, 10th, 13th and 16th month from the start of the relevant chargeable accounting period.'

3   FIONA BANKS

> **Tutorial note.** Remember firstly capital losses are offset against the highest taper relief percentage. Secondly taper relief is applied then the annual exemption is deducted from the total tapered gain.
>
> Marks are maximised by completing the requirement, instead of stopping at taxable gain CGT rates need to be applied. To calculate how much basic rate band left, taxable income must be deducted from £32,400. Remember taxable income is income after the personal allowance is subtracted from the statutory total income figures given in the question.

(a) **CGT payable 2005/06**

Summary

	Business 7 years, 25% £	Non-business 6 years, 80% £
Factory (W1)	54,760	
Painting (W2)		6,383
Less: loss b/f		(3,400)
Net gains	54,760	2,983
Gains after taper relief	13,690	2,386

Note. Loss used against gain with highest taper relief percentage (ie largest amount remaining chargeable) first.

	£
Total gains (13,690 + 2,386)	16,076
Less: annual exemption	(8,500)
Taxable gains	7,576

Basic rate band left

£32,400 − £(34,720 − 4,895) = £2,575

Tax

	£
£2,575 × 20% =	515
£5,001 × 40% =	2,000
£7,576	2,515

Workings

1   Factory

	£
Proceeds	228,000
Less: indexed cost	(138,240)
Less: enhancement	(35,000)
Gain before taper relief	54,760

The factory has been owned for seven complete years, so 25% of the gain will remain chargeable after taper relief.

2   Painting – chattel

	£
Proceeds	9,870
Less: 10% auctioneers fees	(987)
	8,883
Less: cost	(2,500)
Gain before taper relief	6,383

Cannot exceed $\frac{5}{3} \times £(9,870 - 6,000) = £6,450$

Lower amount chosen   £6,383

The painting has been owned for six complete years, therefore 80% of the gain will remain chargeable after taper relief.

(b) (i)   **Chargeable gain**

	£
Proceeds (ie compensation)	29,500
Less: Cost	(18,000)
Gain	11,500
Gain immediately chargeable £(29,500 – 28,000)	(1,500)
Deduction from base cost	10,000

The asset was owned for five complete years, so 85% remains chargeable after taper relief.

Gain (amount not reinvested) £1,500 × 85% = £1,275

(ii)   **Base cost of replacement**

	£
Cost	28,000
Less: deduction from base cost	(10,000)
	18,000

(c) **Principle private residence**

Dates	Actual occupation (months)	Deemed occupation (months)	Non-occupation (months)	Reason
1.7.85 – 31.8.87	26			Lived in
1.9.87 – 30.4.92		56		Any period during which owner required by employment to live abroad
1.5.92 – 31.12.92	8			Lived in
1.1.93 – 31.12.96		48		Up to 4 years during which owner required by employment to live elsewhere UK
1.1.97 – 31.12.97		12		Up to 3 years for any reason provided sandwiched by actual occupation
1.1.98 – 28.2.00	26			Lived in
1.3.00 – 30.6.02			28	
1.7.02 – 30.6.05		36		Last 36 months of ownership deemed as occupied

Marking guide

			Marks	
(a)	Factory		2	
	Taper relief 25%		1	
	Painting – normal gain		1½	
	Painting chattel		1½	
	Taper relief 80%		1	
	Offset of capital loss b/f		1	
	Annual exemption		½	
	CGT calculation		1½	
				10
(b)	(i)	Chargeable gain	2	
		Taper relief 85%	1	
				3
	(ii)	Base cost	1	
(c)	26m occupied		1	
	56m deemed		1	
	8m occupied		1	
	48m deemed		1	
	12m deemed		1	
	26m occupied		1	
	28m non-occupied		1	
	36m occupied		1	
				8
				22

What the examiner said

'This was a three-part question on CGT, involving basic calculations, compensation receipts and principal private residence (PPR) rules.

Part (a) was attempted well, and it is pleasing to note than many candidates now seemed to have grasped the basic rules of calculating simple gains and the resulting capital gains tax.

The most common errors here were not calculating the alternative marginal relief calculation on the painting and actioning taper relief before allocating the losses brought forward to the gain with the least taper entitlement.

Part (b) required candidates to calculate the gain taxable on the receipt of compensation where some of it was not reinvested. The amount of compensation not reinvested is taxed immediately and the remaining gain is then to reduce the base cost of the replacement. Very few candidate were able to demonstrate knowledge of this area.

Part (c) required candidates to produce a table giving dates and reasons why certain periods of time were either occupied, deemed occupied or empty for PPR reasons. Unfortunately this part of the question was very poorly answered. Candidates MUST produce a table where asked and MUST give reasons when asked if they are to score full marks. Many candidates simply copied down dates from the question without any explanation.

The main deemed occupation periods are:

• any period working abroad
• maximum periods of up to four years working elsewhere in UK
• maximum periods of 3 years for any reason

providing that there is an actual period of occupation both before and after those periods.

In addition the last three years of ownership also counts as deemed occupation.'

4   SUSAN CHANCE

> **Tutorial note.** Ensure you only answer the requirement set. Part (a) asks for a description of the loss off-set options available, not advice on which to take. Parts (b) and (c) test specific VAT rules. Writing about other penalties such as late filing penalties for income tax computations or the test for compulsory VAT registration will not score any marks.

(a)

A Technician
1 Main Road
Anyville

Miss Susan Chance
2 Roman Road
Anyville   [Date]

Dear Susan

Off-set of trading loss

Thank you for your query about the options available to off set your £15,000 trading loss in 2004/05.

Years in which the loss can be used

(i)   The loss can be off-set in the same tax year that it was made (ie 2004/05) under a current year claim, or

(ii)   The loss can be off-set in the previous tax year (ie 2003/04) under a 12 month carry back claim, or

(iii)   The loss can be carried forward and off-set against future trading profits from the same trade.

Income it can be used against

(i)   The current year off-set is against the statutory total income (STI) of 2004/05 (ie £4,000).

(ii)   The carry back off-set is against STI of 2003/04 (ie £20,500).

(iii)   The carry forward off-set is against future trading profits of £3,400 in 2005/06.

Claims

The current year claim (i) and carry back claim (ii) are optional. Therefore if you wish to make a claim you must do so to the Revenue before 31 January 2008 stating which year and in which order. The amount of loss off-set is determined by the lower of STI and amounts of the loss.

The carry forward (iii) is automatic and compulsory for any loss remaining so no claim needs to be made. The amount of loss off-set is the lower of future trading profit and amount of the remaining loss.

Three planning points

The following three factors will help you identify the best loss off-set.

1   Obtain the tax relief as soon as possible
2   Save tax at the highest possible rate
3   Avoid wasting your personal allowance

I hope this information has been helpful. If you any further queries please do not hesitate to contact me.

Yours sincerely

A Technician

(b) **Later registration penalty for VAT**

Later registration penalty is based on the net VAT due from the date Monty should have been registered to the date when notification is made.

The rate varies as follows.

	% of net VAT due
Up to 9 months	5
Over 9 months, up to 18 months late	10
Over 18 months late	15

A minimum penalty of £50 applies.

(c) **Tax point for VAT**

The basic tax point is the date goods are delivered. However if prior to this date either;
- an invoice is issued, or
- payment is received then the earlier date becomes the actual tax point.

If the VAT invoice is issued within 14 days after the basic tax point (and an earlier date – as indicated above – does not apply) then the invoice date becomes the tax point.

Tax points in this case are as follows.

£350 deposit   -   14 May 2005 (payment received)

Balance   -   20 July 2005 (invoice issued within 14 days of basic tax point of 16 July 2005)

Marking guide

		Marks
(a)	Presentation	2
	Current year	2
	Carry back	2
	Carry forward	1
	3 planning points	3
		10
(b)	% of net VAT due	1
	Time limits	1½
	Percentages	1½
	Minimum £50	1
		5
(c)	Basic tax point	3
	Actual tax point	1
	Deposit	1
	Balance	1
		6
		21

What the examiner said

'This required knowledge of income tax losses and VAT. This was the worst attempted question on the paper with very few candidates showing much understanding of any of the three areas tested.

Part (a) asked for a letter to a client advising of the use of an income tax loss. Most candidates scored marks for presentation but few scored marks for much more. When giving advice on the use of losses candidates must quote the relevant tax years, the income it can be used against and the amount that must be used. Many candidates quoted wrong section numbers, confusingly using the corporation tax section numbers rather than the income tax ones. Marks are not awarded or lost for section numbers but candidates should try not to use them if they are not sure of the correct ones.

Part (b) asked for details on late notification penalties. These are the only penalties on the syllabus and candidates are required to know the amounts of such penalties but will never be required to calculate an exact figure. Few, if any, knew these amounts.

Part (c) requested candidates to state the tax point for a VAT transaction. This is basic knowledge and vital to the correct administration of VAT. Despite this few candidates could describe the basic rule of the tax point being usually the earliest of delivery, invoice or payment. Where there is a deposit and a final payment then this basic rule is applied to the two payments separately and will result in two different tax points.'

Preparing taxation computations
December 2005

Question Paper	
Time allowed	**3 hours**
ALL FOUR questions are compulsory and MUST be attempted	

Advanced Level
Paper 9

DO NOT OPEN THIS PAPER UNTIL YOU ARE READY TO START
UNDER EXAMINATION CONDITIONS

ALL four questions are compulsory and MUST be attempted.

1 HARRY KNOWLES

Your name is Harry Knowles and you work as a tax technician for a small tax partnership, Pay and Payne.

Your firm has just taken on three new clients: Newco Ltd and two individuals both of whom work for Newco Ltd.

Your line manager has asked you to deal with the following queries, one from each of the new clients.

(a) Newco Ltd is a recently formed company and is due to make up its first set of accounts for the period 1 April 2005 to 31 March 2006. It is aware of the need to complete certain forms as part of the end of year pay as you earn (PAYE) procedures in respect of its employees.

Required:

Write a letter to the Board of Directors of Newco Ltd, giving details of the year end forms required to be completed under the PAYE procedures and stating by what date(s) these forms need to be submitted to HMRC.

For the purposes of this part of the question, assume that today's date is 1 March 2006.

Marks will be awarded for the style and presentation of your answer.   (8 marks)

(b) Sami Jenkins, an employee of Newco Ltd, has asked for help in calculating the value of the benefits she is receiving from Newco Ltd. She has provided the following information regarding the benefits received during the tax year 2005/06:

(i) A loan to help her purchase a new home. Newco Ltd advanced £25,000 on 6 June 2005 at an interest rate of 2% per year. Sami repaid £10,000 on 6 December 2005. The remaining £15,000 was still outstanding on 5 April 2006.

(ii) During the year Newco Ltd paid £3,500 into Sami's personal pension plan.

(iii) Assistance with relocation costs from the Newco Ltd office in Manchester to the Newco Ltd office in Winchester (a distance of 210 miles), totalling £9,500.

(iv) Private medical insurance cover, at an annual cost to the company of £560. If Sami had arranged this cover herself it would have cost her £750.

(v) Workplace parking costing £400.

Sami earns a salary of £28,000 per year.

Required:

Calculate the total value of Sami's benefits to be assessed to income tax for the tax year 2005/06. Clearly identify any benefits which are exempt from tax and, where applicable, include any alternative calculations in full as part of your workings.   (9 marks)

(c) Jenny Smith, another employee of Newco Ltd, who returned to the UK at the end of April 2005, having spent the previous six months on holiday overseas, has asked you to calculate her income tax payable for the tax year 2005/06. She has provided the following information:

(i) She started work with Newco Ltd on 1 May 2005 with an annual salary of £32,700. She received a salary increase of 4% from 1 January 2006.

(ii) A Christmas bonus of £3,000 was received in December 2005 and an end of year bonus of £2,500 in respect of the company's year 1 April 2005 to 31 March 2006 was received in May 2006.

(iii) A taxable benefit of £2,550 has been calculated for the private use of a car provided to her by the company.

(iv) UK dividends of £1,800 (cash amount) were received in January 2006.

(v) Net bank interest of £480 was received in December 2005.

(vi) Premium bond prizes of £250 and £50 were received in May 2005 and November 2005 respectively.

(vii) An amount of £234 was paid to a registered UK charity under the gift aid scheme in November 2005.

(viii) Newco Ltd deducted income tax under PAYE totalling £5,820 from Jenny's earnings.

(ix) A UK property was rented out fully furnished at a monthly rent of £400 from 1 July 2005. The full amount of rent due has been received during 2005/06. Expenses consisted of:

	£
Water rates (for the period 1 April 2005 to 31 March 2006)	240
Repairs to property in January 2006	640
Insurance (for the period 1 April 2005 to 31 March 2006)	360
Agent's fees	510
Cost of new kitchen units	1,800

The property was not available for letting prior to 1 July 2005.

Jenny intends to claim any allowances available.

Required:

Calculate the income tax payable by Jenny for the tax year 2005/06. (18 marks)

(35 marks)

2 RED LTD, BLUE LTD AND GREEN LTD

(a) Red Ltd is a UK resident company with no associates. Red Ltd has always make up accounts to 31 October.

During the year to 31 October 2005 the company had the following transactions in capital items.

Purchases

4 November 2004	Plant costing £6,400
2 May 2005	Plant costing £22,500
8 June 2005	Car (A) costing £20,000
12 July 2005	Car (B) in part exchange (see details below)

Disposals:

3 March 2005	Plant for £8,000 (original cost £7,000)
12 July 2005	Car (C) in part exchange (see details below)
14 August 2005	Car (D) for £3,000(original cost £14,000)

Car (A) purchased in June 2005 will be used 40% for business use and 60% for private use by the Finance Director of the company.

Car (C), which had cost £9,000 in September 2003, was traded in against the purchase of car (B). The trade in value was £4,000 and the new car (B) was worth £11,000. The company paid the additional amount in cash. Car (B) is used 100% for business purposes.

None of the cars are low emission vehicles.

The tax written down value of the general pool of plant and machinery for capital allowance purposes as at 1 November 2004 was £46,000 and the tax written down value of car (D), an expensive car, at the same date was £8,000.

The company is classed as small for capital allowance purposes.

Required:

Calculate the maximum capital allowances that Red Ltd can claim for the year ended 31 October 2005. (10 marks)

(b) Blue Ltd is a UK resident company with no associates. The company has recently changed its accounting year end to September. The company has had the following results for the four accounting periods ending 30 September 2005:

	Year to 31 December 2002 £	9 months to 30 September 2003 £	Year to 30 September 2004 £	Year to 30 September 2005 £
Trading profit	70,000	80,000	–	40,000
Trading loss	–	–	(180,000)	–
Property business income	12,000	9,000	12,000	12,000
Chargeable gain	–	10,000	–	–
Gift aid payment	(2,000)	(2,000)	(2,000)	(2,000)

Required:

(i)   Calculate the profit chargeable to corporation tax (PCTCT) for each of the above periods on the assumption that Blue Ltd claims relief for the trading loss at the earliest opportunity.

(8 marks)

(ii)   State the amounts of any unrelieved losses and/or charges carried forward as at 30 September 2005.

(2 marks)

(c)   Green Ltd is a UK resident company with one 100% owned associate. The company had the following results for the year ended 31 March 2006.

Income

	£
Adjusted trading profit	980,000
Debenture interest received (note 1)	7,500
Chargeable gain	85,000
UK dividends received (not from the associate)	27,000

Expenditure:	
Bank interest paid (note 2)	3,000
Gift aid payment	4,000

Notes:

1.   The debenture interest received was in respect of £100,000 debentures purchased on 16 May 2003 at an interest rate of 10%. The amount of the debenture interest outstanding at 31 March 2006 will be received in April 2006.

2.   The bank interest paid is the full amount due on a loan used to purchase investment.

(6 marks)

Required:

Calculate corporation tax payable by Green Ltd for the year ended 31 March 2006.

(26 marks)

3   NIGEL, JOHN AND PAMELA

(a)   Nigel Hawksworth made the following disposals of capital items in the tax year 2005/06.

14 May 2005: An antique vase was sold for £5,400. The vase had originally cost £3,600 in September 2003.

16 October 2005: A house, which had never been used as Nigel's main residence, was sold for £240,000. The house had originally been purchased in July 1990 for £110,000.The indexed cost of the house on 6 April 1998 was £140,000.

9 January 2006: 3,500 shares in ABC plc were sold for £9,800. Nigel had purchased ABC plc shares at the following times:

May 2003	1,000 shares costing £1,600
August 2004	2,000 shares costing £3,600
May 2005	1 for 2 rights issue taken up, costing £2.20 per share

None of the above assets were classed as business assets.

Required:

Calculate Nigel's total chargeable gains (before the annual exemption) for the tax year 2005/06.

(10 marks)

(b)   Nigel's brother John also made chargeable gains in the tax year 2005/06. His gains (before taper relief) were:

£12,000 is respect of a non-business asset owned for five complete years.
£14,000 in respect of a business asset owned for three complete years.
£3,000 in respect of a non-business asset owned for four complete years.

John also made an allowable capital loss of £5,000 on the sale of a fourth asset in the tax year 2005/06.

John's taxable income (after his personal allowance) for income tax purposes was £29,500 for the tax year 2005/06.

Required:

Calculate the capital gains tax payable by John for the tax year 2005/06.   (7 marks)

(c)   Nigel's sister, Pamela, has her own pottery business. On 1 September 2005 she sold a shop for £80,000, which has cost her £42,000 on 1 May 2000.

In June 2005 she had purchased a new shop for £72,000.

Both shops were used 100% for business purposes.

Required:

On the assumption that Pamela always claims any reliefs available:

(i)   Calculate her chargeable gain (before the annual exemption) on the disposal of the old shop; and   (4 marks)

(ii) State the base cost of the replacement shop for capital gains tax purposes.

(1 mark)

(22 marks)

4   IMOGEN, FREDA AND SEBASTIAN

(a)   Imogen Tombay runs a small sole trader business and is registered for VAT. During the three month period ended 31 October 2005, Imogen carried out the following transactions:

	£
Purchases of stock (exclusive of VAT)	42,000
Sales (exclusive of VAT where applicable):	
Standard rated	98,000
Zero-rated	24,000
Expenses (inclusive of VAT where applicable):	
Wages	8,000
Electricity	1,100
Accounting fees	500
Computer expenses	140

All sales are made with an offer of a 5% discount if settled within 21 days. Only 80% of sales are actually settled within this period.

Imogen wrote off two trade bad debts during the period. One for £300 was due to be paid on 2 January 2005 and the other for £400 was due to be paid on 18 July 2005. Both figures are stated exclusive of VAT.

Imogen does not use either the flat rate scheme or the cash accounting scheme.

Required:

Calculate the VAT payable or reclaimable by Imogen for the three month period ended 31 October 2005, stating by when the VAT return must be submitted.   (8 marks)

(b)   Imogen's sister Freda is also a sole trader and makes her accounts up to 31 March annually. Her profit and loss account for the year ended 31 March 2006 was as follows:

	£	£
Gross profit		260,000
Bank interest received		7,500
Expenses:		
Wages (Note 1)	32,000	
Electricity (Note 2)	2,400	
Rent	1,600	
Computer expenses (Note 3)	860	
Insurance (Note 2)	540	
Drawings by Freda	34,500	
Accounting fees	500	(72,400)
Net profit		195,100

Notes:

1.   The wages figure includes £8,500 for Freda's son who worked only three hours a week for the whole of the year ended 31 March 2006. The normal rate for these duties is £5 per hour.

2.   The electricity and insurance both include private use of 20%.

3.   Freda uses the computer at home for private work and estimates this to be 25% of the total usage.

4.   Freda's capital allowances claim for the year is £2,500.

Required:

Calculate Freda's adjusted trading profit for the year ended 31 March 2006.   (6 marks)

(c)   Imogen's brother Sebastian has previously run a sole trader business but due to falling profits decided to cease trading on 31 March 2006. His adjusted profits for his final three accounting periods were as follows:

Year to 31 October 2004   £12,000
Year to 31 October 2005   £8,000
5 months to 31 March 2006   £3,000

Unused overlap profits from the opening years of his business amounted to £6,000.

Required:

Calculate Sebastian's trading income assessments for all of the tax years affected by the above results.   (3 marks)

(17 marks)

**MOCK EXAM 2
ANSWERS**

DO NOT TURN THIS PAGE UNTIL YOU
HAVE COMPLETED MOCK EXAM 2

WARNING! APPLYING THE MARKING SCHEME

If you decide to mark your paper using the marking scheme (reproduced at the end of each BPP suggested solution), you should bear in mind the following points.

1   The BPP solutions are not definitive: you will see that we have applied our own interpretation of the marking scheme to our solutions to show how good answers should gain marks, but there may be more than one way to answer the question. You must try to judge fairly whether different points made in your answers are correct and relevant and therefore worth marks according to the marking scheme.

2   In numerical answers, do not penalise yourself too much for minor arithmetical errors: if you have followed the correct principles you should gain most of the marks. This emphasises the importance of including workings, which show the marker which principles you were following.

3   If you have a friend or colleague who is studying or has studied this paper, you might ask him or her to mark your paper for you, thus gaining a more objective assessment. Remember you and your friend are not trained or objective markers, so try to avoid complacency or pessimism if you appear to have done very well or very badly.

1   HARRY KNOWLES

Tutorial note. Do note that form P45 is irrelevant in respect of this question.

(a)
                                        Pay and Payne
                                        1 High Street
                                        Newtown

The Board of Directors
Newco Ltd
Waring Industrial Estate
Newtown

                                                        1 March 2006

Dear Sirs

PAYE procedures

In this letter I will set out the PAYE forms that will need to be prepared for the tax year ending 5 April 2006.

Each employee must be provided with a Form P60. This shows total taxable earnings for the year, tax deducted, code number, National Insurance number and the employer's name and address. It must be provided by 31 May 2006.

The same details also need to be shown on the End of Year Return P14. This must be sent to HMRC by 19 May 2006. Also required by HMRC by this date is Form P35 which is a summary of tax and National Insurance deducted.

Finally, for each employee you must provide Form P11D which shows benefits for directors and employees paid £8,500 pa (or Form P9D for other employees). These must be provided by 6 July 2006 to HMRC and each employee.

Please let me know if you have any further queries.

Yours sincerely

A Technician

(b) **Sami Jenkins – Taxable benefits 2005/06**

	£
Taxable cheap loan (W1)	525
Personal pension contribution (N1)	0
Relocation costs (W2)	1,500
Private medical insurance (N2)	560
Work place parking (N3)	0
Total taxable benefits	2,585

Notes

1   Employer contributions to personal pension shares are not taxable benefits.

2   The taxable benefit of the insurance is the cost to the employer of providing the benefit.

3   Workplace parking is an exempt benefit.

Workings

1   Taxable cheap loan

   Average method

   $$\frac{25,000 + 15,000}{2} = £20,000$$

   $$£20,000 \times (5-2)\% \times \frac{10}{12} = \underline{500}$$

Strict method

	£
6.6.05 – 5.12.05	
$6/12 \times £25,000 \times (5 - 2)\%$	375
6.12.05 – 5.4.06	
$4/12 \times £15,000 \times (5 - 2)\%$	150
	525

Sami should not elect for the strict method. HMRC may do so and it has been assumed that it will do so, even though the difference is small.

2   Relocation

	£
Costs	9,500
Less: exempt	(8,000)
Taxable benefit	1,500

(c) **Jenny Smith – Income tax payable 2005/06**

	Non-savings income	Savings (excl. dividend) income	Dividend income	Total income
	£	£	£	£
Salary (W1)	30,302			
Bonus – receipts basis	3,000			
Car benefits	2,550			
Dividends £1,800 × 100/90			2,000	
BI £480 × 100/80		600		
Property business income (W2)	1,658			
STI	37,510	600	2,000	40,110
Less: Personal allowance	(4,895)			
Taxable income	32,615	600	2,000	35,215

Note Premium bond winnings exempt from income tax.

	£
£2,090 × 10%	209
£30,310 × 22%	6,668
£215 × 22% (gift aid)	47
£(300 – 215) = 85 × 20% (gift aid)	17
£(600 – 85) = 515 × 40%	206
£2,000 × 32½%	650
	7,797

	£	
Less: PAYE	5,820	
BI £600 × 20%	120	
Dividend credit £2,000 × 10%	200	
		(6,140)
		1,657

Workings

1   Salary

	£
1.5.05 – 31.12.05	
32,700 × 8/12	21,800
1.1.06 – 31.3.06	
32,700 × 104% × 3/12	8,502
	30,302

2 Property business income

		£	£
Rent:	£400 × 9		3,600
Less:	Water rates		
	240 ×9/12	180	
	Repairs	640	
	Insurance		
	360 × 9/12	270	
	Agents fees	510	
	Wear and tear		
	£(3,600 – 180) × 10%	342	(1,942)
	Property business income 2005/06		1,658

Note: Kitchen units are a capital expense and so not deductible.

3 Gift aid donation

£234 × 100/78   300

Extend the basic rate band by this amount.

Marking guide

		Marks
(a)	Layout	2
	P60	2
	P14	1
	P35	1
	P11D/P9D	2
		8
(b)	Taxable cheap loan	4
	Personal pension	1
	Relocation	1½
	Private medical insurance	1
	Workplace parking	1
	Total taxable benefits	1½
		9
(c)	Salary	2
	Bonus	1
	Car benefit	½
	Dividends	1
	Bank interest	1
	Property business income – Rental	1
	Water rates	1
	Repairs	½
	Insurance	1
	Agents fees	½
	Wear and tear	1½
	Kitchen units	½
	PA	½
	Premium bond prizes	1
	Starting rate band	½
	Basic rate band	1
	Gift aid	1
	Savings income	½
	Dividend income	½
	PAYE	½
	BI	½
	Dividend	½
		18
		35

2 RED LTD, BLUE LTD AND GREEN LTD

> **Tutorial note.**
>
> - It is best in part (b) for your presentation to use a four column table as shown in the model answer and as indicated by the layout of the question.
>
> - Don't forget to divide the upper and lower limits by the two associated companies.

(a) **Red Ltd – Maximum capital allowance y/e 31 October 2005**

	FYA £	Pool £	Car A £	Car D £	Allowances £
TWDV b/f		46,000		8,000	
Disposals					
3.3.05 Plant (restrict to cost)		(7,000)			
12.7.05 Car C		(4,000)			
14.8.05 Car D				(3,000)	
Balancing allowance				5,000	5,000
		35,000			
Additions not qualifying for FYA					
8.6.05 Car A (N)			20,000		
12.7.05 Car B		11,000			
		46,000			
WDA @ 25%/maximum		(11,500)	(3,000)		14,500
		34,500			
Additions qualifying for FYA					
4.11.04 Plant	6,400				
FYA @ 50%	(3,200)	3,200			3,200
2.5.05 Plant	22,500				
FYA @ 40%	(9,000)	13,500			9,000
TWDV c/f		51,200	17,000		
Allowances					31,700

Note. No restriction for private use by employee on company. Taxable benefit for director.

(b) (i) **Blue Ltd – PCTCT**

	Y/e 31.12.02 £	P/e 30.9.03 £	Y/e 30.9.04 £	Y/e 30.9.05 £
Trading profit	70,000	80,000	0	40,000
Less: S.393 (1) loss relief				(40,000)
				0
Property business income	12,000	9,000	12,000	12,000
Chargeable gain		10,000		
	82,000	99,000	12,000	12,000
Less: S.393A (1)	(20,500)	(99,000)	(12,000)	0
	61,500	0	0	12,000
Less: gift aid	(2,000)	0	0	(2,000)
PCTCT	59,500	0	0	10,000

Loss memorandum

		£
Loss: y/e 30.9.04		180,000
Less: S.393A (1)	– c/y	(12,000)
	- p/e 30.9.03	(99,000)
	- y/e 31.12.02	
	3/12× £82,000 (N)	(20,500)
s.393 (1) c/f		(40,000)
Unrelieved loss		8,500

Note. Only 3 months of the year to 31.12.02 fall within the 12 months prior to the year of the loss.

(ii) The gift aid donations cannot be relieved for p/e 30.9.03 and y/e 30.9.04. They cannot be carried forward as they are non-trade charges.

The unrelieved trade loss at 30.9.05 is £8,500.

(c) **Green Ltd – Corporation tax y/e 31 March 2006**

	£	£
Trading profit		980,000
- debenture interest accrued £100,000 × 10%	10,000	
- bank interest paid for non-trade purposes	(3,000)	7,000
Capital gain		85,000
		1,072,000
Less: gift aid (charge)		(4,000)
PCTCT		1,068,000
Add: FII £27,000 × 100/90		30,000
"Profits"		1,098,000

Small companies marginal relief limits:

Lower limit $\frac{300,000}{2}$ = 150,000

Upper limit $\frac{1,500,000}{2}$ = 750,000

Full rate applies
£1,068,000 × 30% = 320,400

Marking guide

		Marks	
(a)	Plant disposal – restrict to cost	1	
	Car C disposal	1	
	Car D	½	
	Car A	1½	
	Car B	1	
	WDA	2	
	Plant	1	
	FYAS	2	10
(b) (i)	Trading Profit	1	
	Loss c/f	1½	
	Property business income	1	
	Loss c/y	1	
	Loss c/b – p/e 30.9.03	½	
	y/e 31.12.02	2	
	Gift aid p/e 30.9.03, y/e 31.12.02	1	8
(ii)	Gift aid unrelieved	1	
	Loss unrelieved	1	2
(c)	Trading profit	½	
	Investment income	1½	
	Gain	½	
	Charge	½	
	FII	1	
	SCR limits	1	
	CT payable	1	6
			26

3 NIGEL, JOHN AND PAMELA

> **Tutorial note.**
> - For part (a) don't forget that proceeds and cost <£6,000 therefore EXEMPT.
> - In part (b) do practice the offset of a capital loss before applying taper relief, as it nearly in every sitting of the exam.

(a) **Nigel – total chargeable gains 2005/06**

	£
Vase (W1)	0
House (W2)	70,000
Shares (W2) – August 2004	2,600
May 2003	500
Gains 2005/06 (before AE)	73,100

Workings

1 Vase

Proceeds of £6,000 or less – exempt chattel

2 House

	£
Proceeds	240,000
Less: indexed cost	(140,000)
Indexed gain	100,000

Taper relief ownership period (6.4.98 – 5.4.05 = 7 years plus bonus year for non-business asset)

Gain after taper relief (70%)	70,000

3 Shares

Last in, first out basis

August 2004

	No.	Cost £
Acquisition	2,000	3,600
Rights 1:2 @ £2.20	1,000	2,200
	3,000	5,800
Sale	(3,000)	(5,800)
C/f	0	0

Gain

	£
Proceeds $\frac{3,000}{3,500} \times £9,800$	8,400
Less: cost	(5,800)
Gain	2,600

No taper relief – sold within 3 years.

May 2003

	No.	Cost £
Acquisition	1,000	1,600
Rights 1:2 @ £2.20	500	1,100
	1,500	2,700
Sale	(500)	(900)
C/f	1,000	1,800

Gain

		£
Proceeds $\dfrac{500}{3,500} \times 9,800$		1,400
Less: cost		(900)
Gain		500

No taper relief – sold within 3 years.

(b) **John – CGT payable 2005/06**

	Business	*Non-business*	
	2+years	*5 yrs*	*4 yrs*
	£	£	£
Gains	14,000	12,000	3,000
Less: loss (best use)		(2,000)	(3,000)
Gains before taper relief	14,000	10,000	0

Gains after taper relief

	£
$14,000 \times 25\%$	3,500
$10,000 \times 85\%$	8,500
	12,000
Less: AE	(8,500)
Taxable gains	3,500

Basic rate band remaining:

	£
$(32,400 - 29,500) = 2,900 \times 20\%$	580
$(3,500 - 2,900) = 600 \times 40\%$	240
CGT payable 2005/06	820

(c) (i) **Pamela gain on shop**

	£
Proceeds	80,000
Less: cost	(42,000)
Gain	38,000

Immediately chargeable = amount not reinvested in new shop.

	£
£(80,000 – 72,000)	8,000
Taper relief ownership period (1.1.2000 – 1.9.2005) = 5 years	
Gain after taper relief (25%)	2,000
Gain rolled over £(38,000 – 8,000)	30,000

(ii) Base cost of new shop

	£
Cost	72,000
Less: rolled over gain	(30,000)
Base cost for CGT	42,000

Marking guide

			Marks
(a)	Vase		1
	House - gain		1
	- after taper relief		1
	- net gain		1
	Shares – *August 2004*		
	Cost		2
	Gain		1
	May 2003		
	Cost		2
	Gain		1
	Taper relief position		1½
	Summary		½
			10
(b)	Use of loss		2
	gains after taper		2
	AE		1
	Basic rate tax		1
	Higher rate tax		1
			7
(c)	(i) Gain		1
	Chargeable		1
	Taper relief		1
	Rolled over gain		1
			4
	(ii) Base cost		1
			22

4 IMOGEN, FREDA AND SEBASTIAN

Tutorial note.

- In part (a) make sure you understand the difference between VAT inclusive and exclusive amounts. Learn the date the VAT payment and return is due.

- In part (b) always start with the net profit and add back the disallowed amounts.

- In part (c) note that the business has CEASED - it is therefore the closing year rules that are being tested here.

(a) **Imogen – VAT return q/e 31 October 2005**

	£
Output VAT	
Sales 98,000 × 95% = 93,100 × 17.5% (N1)	16,292
Input VAT	
Stock 42,000 × 17.5%	(7,350)
Electricity (N3) 1,100 × 7/47	(164)
Accounting fees 500 × 7/47	(74)
Computer expenses 140 × 7/47	(21)
Bad debt (N4) 300 × 17.5%	(52)
VAT payable	8,631

Return due one month after end of period ie by 30 November 2005.

Notes.

1   VAT chargeable on net amount regardless of whether discount taken up
2   Wages not within VAT
3   Reduced rate of VAT only applies to domestic fuel.
4   Bad debt relief available to debts over 6 months old only.

(b)   **Freda – Trading profit y/e 31 March 2006**

		£
Net profit as in accounts		195,100
Add:	Excess wages to son (W)	7,720
	Private electricity 2,400 × 20%	480
	Private computer use 860 × 25%	215
	Private insurance 540 × 20%	108
	Drawings by Freda	34,500
		238,123
Less: bank interest (taxable as savings income)		(7,500)
Capital allowances		(2,500)
Adjusted trading profit		228,123

Working

	£
Wages paid to son	8,500
Less: wages usually payable 52 × 3 × £5	(780)
Excess wages (not wholly trade purpose)	7,720

(c)   **Sebastian – 2004/05 and 2005/06 trading income assessments**

	£	£
2004/05		
y/e 31.10.04		12,000
2005/06		
Y/e 31.10.05	8,000	
P/e 31.3.06	3,000	
	11,000	
Less: overlap profits	(6,000)	5,000

Marking guide

		Marks
(a)	Sales	$1\frac{1}{2}$
	Stock	1
	Electricity	1
	Accountancy	1
	Computer	1
	Bad debt	1
	Net VAT due	$\frac{1}{2}$
	VAT return date	$\underline{1}$
		8
(b)	Net profit	$\frac{1}{2}$
	Excess wages	1
	Private electricity	1
	Private computer use	1
	Private insurance	1
	Drawings	$\frac{1}{2}$
	Bank interest	$\frac{1}{2}$
	Capital allowances	$\underline{\frac{1}{2}}$
		6
(c)	2004/05	1
	2005/06 – y/e 31.10.05	$\frac{1}{2}$
	p/e 31.3.06	$\frac{1}{2}$
	Overlap profits	$\underline{1}$
		$\underline{3}$
		$\underline{\underline{17}}$

Tax Rates and Allowances

The following tax rates and allowances are to be used in answering the questions.

Income tax

Starting rate	£1 – £2,090	10%
Basic rate	£2,091 – £32,400	22%
Higher rate	£32,401 and above	40%

Note

UK dividends will be taxed at 10% when they fall within the basic rate band and 32.5% thereafter.

Personal allowance

Personal allowance under 65	£4,895

Company car benefit

Base level for CO_2 emissions: 140 grams per kilometre

Car fuel benefit

Base figure £14,400

Approved mileage allowances

All cars:

Up to 10,000 miles	40p
Over 10,000 miles	25p

Official rate of interest

5%

Personal pension contribution limits

Age	Maximum percentage
up to 35	17.5
36–45	20
46–50	25
51–55	30
56–60	35
61 or more	40

Subject to earnings cap of £105,600.

Corporation tax

Financial year	2005	2004
Starting rate (SR)	0%	0%
Small companies (SC) rate	19%	19%
Full rate	30%	30%
Starting rate lower limit	£10,000	£10,000
Starting rate upper limit	£50,000	£50,000
Small companies rate – lower limit	£300,000	£300,000
Small companies rate – upper limit	£1,500,000	£1,500,000
Marginal relief fraction:		
Starting rate	19/400	19/400
Small companies rate	11/400	11/400

Profits paid out as dividends to non-corporate shareholders are subject to a minimum rate of corporate tax of 19%.

Marginal relief

$$(M - P) \times I/P \times \text{marginal relief fraction}$$

Tapering relief for capital gains tax

The percentage of the gain chargeable is as follows.

No of complete years after 5 April 1998	Gains on business assets (%)	Gains on non-business assets (%)
0	100	100
1	50	100
2	25	100
3	25	95
4	25	90
5	25	85
6	25	80
7	25	75
8	25	70
9	25	65
10	25	60

Capital gains tax: Annual exemption

Individuals   £8,500

National insurance (not contracted-out rates)

		%
Class 1	£1 – £4,895 per year	Nil
	£4,896 – £32,760 per year	11.0
	£32,761 and above per year	1.0
Class 1 Employer	£1 – £4,895 per year	Nil
	£4,895 and above per year	12.8
Class 2	£2.10 per week	
Class 4	£1 – £4,895 per year	Nil
	£4,896 – £32,760 per year	8.0
	£32,761 and above per year	1.0

Capital allowances

FYA	40%
WDA – Plant and machinery	25%
WDA – Industrial buildings	4%

Notes

For the period from 1 April 2004 to 31 March 2005 (6 April 2004 to 5 April 2005 for unincorporated businesses) the rate of plant and machinery first year allowance is increased to 50% for small businesses.

A FYA of 100% applies for low emission motorcars (CO_2 emissions of less than 120 g/m).

Apportionments

All apportionments should be to the nearest month

Calculations and workings need only be made to the nearest £.

All workings should be shown.

REVIEW FORM & FREE PRIZE DRAW

All original review forms from the entire BPP range, completed with genuine comments, will be entered into one of two draws on 31 July 2006 and 31 January 2007. The names on the first four forms picked out on each occasion will be sent a cheque for £50.

Name: _____   **Address:** _____

_____

Date: _____   _____

How have you used this Practice & Revision Kit?
(Tick one box only)

☐ Home study (book only)

☐ On a course: college _____

☐ With 'correspondence' package

☐ Other _____

Why did you decide to purchase this Practice & Revision Kit? *(Tick one box only)*

☐ Have used complementary Interactive Text

☐ Have used BPP Texts in the past

☐ Recommendation by friend/colleague

☐ Recommendation by a lecturer at college

☐ Saw advertising in journals

☐ Saw website

☐ Other _____

During the past six months do you recall seeing/receiving any of the following?
(Tick as many boxes as are relevant)

☐ Our advertisement in *ACCA Student Accountant*

☐ Other advertisement _____

☐ Our brochure with a letter through the post

Which (if any) aspects of our advertising do you find useful?
(Tick as many boxes as are relevant)

☐ Prices and publication dates of new editions

☐ Information on Practice & Revision Kit content

☐ Facility to order books off-the-page

☐ None of the above

Have you used the companion Interactive Text for this subject?   ☐ Yes   ☐ No

Your ratings, comments and suggestions would be appreciated on the following areas

	Very useful	Useful	Not useful
Introductory section (How to use this Practice & Revision Kit)	☐	☐	☐
'Do You Know' checklists	☐	☐	☐
'Did You Know' checklists	☐	☐	☐
Possible pitfalls	☐	☐	☐
Objective test questions	☐	☐	☐
Short-form questions	☐	☐	☐
Content of answers	☐	☐	☐
Mock exams	☐	☐	☐
Structure & presentation	☐	☐	☐
Icons	☐	☐	☐

	Excellent	Good	Adequate	Poor
Overall opinion of this Kit	☐	☐	☐	☐

Do you intend to continue using BPP Interactive Texts/Kits?   ☐ Yes   ☐ No

Please note any further comments and suggestions/errors on the reverse of this page.

Please return to: Mary Maclean, BPP Professional Education, FREEPOST, London, W12 8BR

REVIEW FORM & FREE PRIZE DRAW (continued)

Please note any further comments and suggestions/errors below

FREE PRIZE DRAW RULES

1   Closing date for 31 July 2006 draw is 30 June 2006. Closing date for 31 January 2007 draw is 31 December 2006.

2   Restricted to entries with UK and Eire addresses only. BPP employees, their families and business associates are excluded.

3   No purchase necessary. Entry forms are available upon request from BPP Professional Education. No more than one entry per title, per person. Draw restricted to persons aged 16 and over.

4   Winners will be notified by post and receive their cheques not later than 6 weeks after the relevant draw date.

5   The decision of the promoter in all matters is final and binding. No correspondence will be entered into.